The Trial of the Scottsboro Boys

THE TRIAL OF THE SCOTTSBORO BOYS

David Aretha

MORGAN REYNOLDS

PUBLISHING

Greensboro, North Carolina

THE CIVIL RIGHTS MOVEMENT

THE TRIAL OF THE SCOTTSBORO BOYS
Copyright © 2008 by David Aretha

Library of Congress Cataloging-in-Publication Data

Aretha, David.
    The trial of the Scottsboro boys / by David Aretha. -- 1st ed.
      p. cm. -- (Civil rights series)
    Includes bibliographical references and index.
    ISBN-13: 978-1-59935-058-5
    ISBN-10: 1-59935-058-0
    1. Scottsboro Trial, Scottsboro, Ala., 1931. 2. Trials (Rape)--Alabama--
Scottsboro. [1. African Americans--Civil rights--History.] I. Title.

    KF224.S34A74 2007
    345.761'9502523--dc22

                                            2007023818

Printed in the United States of America
First Edition

Contents

The nine Scottsboro Boys with attorney Samuel Leibowitz
(*Courtesy of Bettmann/Corbis*)

one

The Train From Chattanooga

O n March 25, 1931, four African American teenagers jumped on a freight car of the Southern Railroad in Chattanooga, Tennessee. It was a chilly but sunny day and the four joined about twenty other men, black and white, on the train as it slowly chugged out of Chattanooga. The train was scheduled to dip south into Alabama before heading north to Memphis, where the four—Haywood Patterson, Eugene Williams, and brothers Roy and Andy Wright—hoped to find work hauling logs on the Mississippi River.

The United States was in the grips of the Great Depression. Millions were unemployed and thousands of men had left their homes and took to riding freight trains—called hoboing—in a desperate attempt to find work. Hoboing was illegal, but lawmen often looked the other way. The young black men hoboing on the train had no way of knowing they would soon be caught up in one of the most tragic examples of racial injustice in American history.

During the Great Depression many people became hobos, riding freight trains in an attempt to find work. *(Library of Congress)*

There were a few other black teens on the freight car, hailing from various parts of Georgia. There were also some white riders, looking for work anywhere they could get it, just like the black youths. Amongst the whites were two young women, Victoria Price and Ruby Bates, returning to Huntsville, Alabama. They had come to Chattanooga in hopes of finding work in the cotton mills, but were returning home, still unemployed and broke.

Victoria Price (left) and Ruby Bates *(Courtesy of Bettmann/Corbis)*

Trouble began when one of the white boys stepped on Patterson's hand and almost pushed Williams off the train. Patterson and Williams remained quiet and did not complain—black Southerners learned from a young age not to challenge white folks—but when the same boy brushed by Williams again and almost pushed him off the train, Patterson spoke up: "The next time you want by, just tell me you want by and I let you by."

"Nigger bastard, this a white man's train," the white boy said. "You better get off. All you black bastards better get off!"

Patterson decided to stand up for himself and his friends, which took an enormous amount of courage in the Jim Crow

South. He insisted that he and his buddies had as much right to ride the train as white people.

"Why, you goddamn nigger, I think we better just put you off!" the white youth responded.

"Okay, you just try," Patterson shot back. "You just try to put us off!"

The white boys muttered and cursed among themselves, then moved to another car. When the train slowed during an uphill climb, the whites jumped off and threw rocks at the black youths, and then climbed back on another car.

When the train stopped in Stevenson, Alabama, the four friends from Chattanooga were joined by other African American riders, and they told them what had happened. After the whites flung more rocks, and the train started up again, the Chattanooga foursome and about eight other black kids confronted their attackers, approximately six or seven white teenagers. Fistfights erupted and the black youths quickly got the upper hand. "We had color anger on our side," remembered Patterson.

As the fight turned against them, some of the white combatants jumped from the train, while others were pushed off. Only one white youngster, Orville Gilley, remained on the car—the black youths spared him because the train had gained too much speed to safely throw him off.

After the white youths were off the train, Patterson and his friends went back to the oil tanker, but the trouble was far from over. Upset at being bested, the white boys hurried to the town of Stevenson, where they complained that the black kids had jumped them and thrown them off the train. One white said he wanted to press charges.

The Scottsboro Boys stand in this photo taken shortly after their arrest. They are (from left to right): Clarence Norris, Olen Montgomery, Andy Wright, Willie Roberson, Ozie Powell, Eugene Williams, Charlie Weems, Roy Wright, and Haywood Patterson. *(Courtesy of Bettmann/Corbis)*

The train was scheduled to stop in Paint Rock, Alabama. A request to arrest the boys was sent to M. L. Wann, sheriff of Jackson County, where Paint Rock was located. Wann, in turn, phoned Deputy Sheriff Charlie Latham and told him to round up every man with a gun he could find.

When the train pulled in to Paint Rock, a large posse of white men was waiting. Pointing shotguns and rifles, the men pulled nine black youngsters from the train: Patterson, Williams, the Wrights, Ozie Powell, Clarence Norris, Charlie Weems, Olen Montgomery, and Willie Roberson. Several other black kids ran away. The men also took Gilley and two young women—Victoria Price and Ruby Bates—from the train.

Fearing for their lives, the nine youths insisted they had not started the trouble. Heedless to their pleas, Latham had them roped together and loaded onto a truck and sent to nearby Scottsboro, Alabama. From this day forward, the nine young men would be known as the Scottsboro Boys.

Haywood Patterson, age nineteen, had been riding the rails for four years. Though illiterate, he was smart and sassy—and the least likely to be intimidated. Twenty-year-old Charlie Weems was the oldest of the nine. His long, sad face reflected his life of hardship. His mother had died when he was four, and only one of his seven siblings survived childhood.

Clarence Norris and Ozie Powell were well-built young men in their late teens. Norris had begun working in the cotton fields at age seven, then toiled up to sixteen hours a day in a Goodyear plant. Powell, quiet and shy, had only one year of schooling. He had worked in a lumber company for several years.

Eugene Williams was a friend of Patterson and the Wright brothers. Barely removed from childhood, the thirteen-year-old Williams was shorter and thinner than the others. Andy Wright, nineteen, had driven a truck since age twelve to support his family because of his father's poor health. For the rest of this day and beyond, Andy did his best to console his little brother, Roy, who was just thirteen years old.

Willie Roberson and Olen Montgomery were plagued with physical handicaps. Roberson suffered badly from syphilis and gonorrhea. With sores on his genitals, he needed a cane to walk. Montgomery was blind in his left eye and could barely see out of his right. All nine of the Scottsboro Boys

A map of Alabama *(Courtesy of the C.I.A. World Factbook)*

had seen hard times, but they were not prepared for what was to come—especially after Ruby Bates's accusation.

After departing the train, Bates and her friend, Victoria Price, chatted with women gathered at the station. The two female hobos wore overalls over dresses and other clothes. Bates was the more timid of the two, but after a few minutes she approached Deputy Sheriff Latham and made an accusation that would send shockwaves throughout the South: The nine black youths, she said, had raped her and Price on the train.

In the Jim Crow South such an accusation was equivalent to a death sentence. Since the Civil War, hundreds of black men had been lynched after being accused—not convicted—of raping a white woman. The thought of a black man having sex with a white woman of the South, forcibly or consensually, infuriated Southern white men. Said South Carolina Governor Ben Tillman in 1892, "Governor as I am, I would lead a mob to lynch the Negro who ravishes a white woman."

In the South, African Americans tempted fate by even looking at a white woman. Said Haywood Baugh of Richmond, Virginia, "[W]hen I was a young man, they had a law that they called 'reckless eyeballing.' If they saw you looking at a white woman, they would arrest you for reckless eyeballing." In 1923, a woman in Rosewood, Florida, said she was raped by a black man and whites responded by killing African Americans and burning down the whole town.

When Bates's accusation spread among the locals, Latham and Sheriff Wann knew they had a "situation" on their hands. Wann sent Bates and Price to Scottsboro to be examined by two physicians. Meanwhile, the nine Scottsboro Boys were locked up in the decrepit county jail. In the late afternoon, farmers from the region began to descend upon the building. By evening, the crowd swelled to several hundred. Vengeful farmers surrounded the jail, with their curious wives and children looking on from nearby.

Sheriff Wann so feared an attack on the jail that he had men barricade the doors from the inside. Mayor James

David Snodgrass pleaded with the people to leave, but the mob demanded that the accused be released so they could be lynched then and there. "The crowd was howling like dogs," Norris wrote, "throwing rocks and threatening to burn us out."

Initially, the Scottsboro Boys were told that they were being held for assault and attempted murder. But while in jail, they were lined up for viewing by Bates and Price. Victoria pointed to six of them. "If those six had Miss Price," a guard declared, "it stands to reason that the others had Miss Bates." When Norris called them liars, a guard responded by stabbing Clarence's hand with a bayonet.

By 8:30 p.m. Wann so feared a rush on the jail that he decided to load the Scottsboro Boys in deputies' cars and transport them to a different jail. But Wann had to scrap the plan when he discovered that none of the cars' headlamps worked. Wires on all three cars had been cut.

With that, Wann phoned Alabama governor Ben Miller, who promptly ordered National Guardsmen to Scottsboro. As twenty-five Guardsmen arrived to break up the crowd, most of the mob departed. Only a few hung around in their cars as bedtime approached.

Inside the jail, the Scottsboro Boys went to bed terrified. "I was scared before, but it wasn't nothing to how I felt now," Norris recalled. "All I could think was that I was going to die for something that I had not done."

Norris and the others were about to become embroiled in one of the most notorious legal cases of the twentieth century—one that would drag on for more than seven years. The single accusation uttered by Ruby Bates would spark a wildfire of litigation, eventually involving the nation's most prominent attorneys, the U.S. Supreme Court twice, and even the president of the United States—while illuminating for all to see the injustice of the Jim Crow South.

two
Jim Crow "Justice"

I n another time or place, the Scottsboro case never would have even gone to trial. After all, Victoria Price and Ruby Bates had departed the train fully dressed and well composed—despite their claim they had just been gang raped. The girls had chatted calmly for several minutes with women from the area before making the accusation. Moreover, medical examinations by two doctors ninety minutes after the alleged rapes revealed no evidence of forced sexual intercourse. Yet when they awoke on March 26, 1931, the Scottsboro Boys faced what seemed to be a certain death. Should they live long enough to make it to trial, the death penalty would surely be their fate.

To comprehend the story of the Scottsboro Boys, it's necessary to understand the history of Jim Crow laws and practices up until 1931. President Abraham Lincoln had issued the Emancipation Proclamation, declaring that all slaves held in the southern states fighting the Civil War would henceforth be free, in 1863. In 1865, Congress passed the Thirteenth Amendment to the Constitution, officially abolishing slavery in the United States.

After losing the Civil War, many southerners vehemently opposed the ending of slavery, and they continued to fume as Congress passed more legislation expanding civil rights. The Fourteenth Amendment, passed in 1868, granted full citizenship to all people born or naturalized in the United States—including freed slaves. The Fifteenth Amendment (1870) guaranteed voting rights to all adult male citizens. In addition, the Civil Rights Act of 1875 prohibited discrimination in public facilities.

During the era of Reconstruction (following the Civil War), federal troops and officials were sent into the South. Among other duties, they oversaw the construction of black schools and ensured that blacks were granted the right to

Hiram Revels became the first black U.S. senator in 1870. *(Library of Congress)*

vote. Some southern blacks were appointed to prominent political positions, including Hiram R. Revels of Mississippi, the first black U.S. senator, in 1870, and P. B. S. Pinchback of Louisiana, the first black governor, also in 1870.

Over time, northern officials hoped that Southerners would acquiesce to the new federal laws and welcome African Americans as fellow citizens. However, they were overly optimistic. Many Southerners considered blacks not just inferior to whites, but subhuman. They were convinced that blacks were hopelessly ignorant and a sexual threat to southern womanhood. Such stereotypes had been perpetuated and entrenched for generations. On a more practical level, Southerners had longed relied on free slave labor, and they could not afford to pay white man's wages to black workers.

The Ku Klux Klan, formed in 1866 in Pulaski, Tennessee, unleashed violence on African Americans. Meanwhile, the U.S. Supreme Court rendered several decisions that undermined Congress's civil rights laws. In 1876, for example, it declared that citizens could be denied the right to vote if they didn't meet certain criteria. Once Reconstruction ended in 1877, when federal troops left the South, blacks in the region fell to the mercy of "southern justice." Southern states and local governments quickly began passing "black codes" forbidding African Americans from basic citizen rights, such as the right to serve on juries, bear arms, rent and own land, drink alcohol, travel, and even learn to read. These acts of discrimination came to be known as the Jim Crow laws, named after a popular song, "Jump Jim Crow," performed by a white man in blackface, mocking blacks.

From the post-Civil War period up to the 1960s, Jim Crow was the rule in the South. As the laws became more

Blacks in the South had separate drinking fountains, among other things, most of which were inferior to what was provided for whites. *(Library of Congress)*

onerous and cruel, they mandated that public facilities, such as streetcars and schools, be segregated to keep blacks away from whites. Almost without exception, the white facilities were superior to the black facilities. Throughout the South, seemingly everything became segregated—from parks and restaurants to outhouses and drinking fountains. Many laws and ordinances were created to keep African Americans "in their place." Blacks had to step off a sidewalk when a white person approached, and black shoppers had to put money on the store counter so as to avoid touching the white store owner's hand.

Through sharecropping, plantation owners kept African Americans economically enslaved. Black sharecroppers

In the Jim Crow South, many public facilities were segregated. *(Library of Congress)*

owed so much to the white landowners—for rent, food, and farming equipment—that they were perpetually in debt. Any black male arrested for even the pettiest infraction could be forced to serve as free labor for a white man.

Jim Crow did not spare black children. In 1930, Alabama spent more than five times more money per student to educate white children. As late as the 1930s, most southern black students didn't attend school for more than twenty weeks per year and were taught by poorly trained teachers using old textbooks in inferior facilities. In the wintertime, black children shivered in drafty shacks that served as schools.

In theory, Americans could correct injustice at the voting booth. But even though the Fifteenth Amendment gave African Americans the right to vote, very few black citizens cast ballots in the Jim Crow South. Deviously, Southern states had passed laws forcing blacks to pay a poll tax or pass "understanding" tests in order to vote. One test included this question: "Name one area of authority over state militia reserved exclusively to the states." (Answer: "The appointment of officers.") Inevitably, African Americans failed these nearly impossible tests and thus were denied the opportunity to vote.

The few black citizens who paid their poll taxes and passed the rigged tests took big risks showing up on Election Day. Those who tried to vote could be fired from their jobs, physically assaulted, or killed. Whites could abuse blacks as they pleased. Even if a white man was put on trial for abusing or killing an African American, he inevitably would be found not guilty by an all-white jury.

Often, whites took "justice" into their own hands. From 1882 through 1930, according to the Tuskegee Institute, 3,386 African Americans were lynched—killed by hanging, shooting, beating, or burning, without benefit of trial. Sometimes, large crowds of whites would arrive for a scheduled lynching, with some bringing their cameras and a picnic lunch.

Well into the twentieth century, the federal government turned a blind eye to injustice in the Jim Crow South. An anti-lynching bill introduced in the U.S. Congress in 1922 never passed. In 1909, the National Association for the Advancement of Colored People (NAACP) was formed to fight for black causes. But up through 1930, it could accomplish little. In fact, the Ku Klux Klan had become a much more powerful force. In the 1920s, the Klan's national membership surged past 4 million, including local and state

The Ku Klux Klan became a powerful organization in the 1920s. In this photo, Klansmen march down Pennsylvania Avenue in Washington, D.C. *(Library of Congress)*

politicians. On August 8, 1925, 40,000 Klansmen marched down Pennsylvania Avenue in Washington, D.C.

Four years later, the stock market crash plunged the nation into an economic depression that would last until the beginning of World War II. Nearly everyone suffered, especially African Americans. While white unemployment soared above 20 percent, black unemployment was more than twice that—up to 50 percent in certain cities. In the South, the slogan was "No jobs for niggers until every white man has a job." It comes as no surprise that the Scottsboro Boys were riding the rails looking for work.

The whites of Scottsboro felt no sympathy for the accused, especially in the heart of the Depression. The town seemed pleasant and prosperous, with wide streets and big lawns shaded by oak trees and Southern sweet gums. More than 90 percent of the county's workers toiled in agriculture—primarily cotton. But a combination of drought and low demand had put a tight pinch on farmers, and they had little money to spend in Scottsboro's stores.

In the days following the arrests, the local newspapers reported the alleged attack as fact. The headline of the *Jackson County Sentinel* blared: "All Negroes Positively Identified by Girls and One White Boy Who Was Held Prisoner with Pistol and Knives While Nine Black Fiends Committed Revolting Crime."

Reporters found a treasure trove in the suddenly chatty Victoria Price, who offered up her life story. Slender with fair skin and short brown hair, the twenty-one-year-old Price told how she had grown up in the Huntsville cotton mill villages. She had to quit school at age ten, and since 1927 had supported both herself and her widowed mother. With her work hours drastically cut, Price and her friend Ruby Bates rode the freight train to Chattanooga days earlier looking for steady work in the cotton mills.

In the coming weeks and months, acquaintances of Price would refer to her as "a common street prostitute of the lowest type" who had sex with both white and black men in her racially mixed neighborhood. She would be called a hard drinker who was prone to fights, and a woman who would "be out at all hours of the night and curse and swear, and be a general nuisance to the negro population."

Yet in the local newspapers in the days after the alleged attack, Price would come across as a vulnerable Southern girl, victimized by bad breaks, hard economic times, and, finally, a gang of black brutes. Price told reporters that on the ride back from Chattanooga, she, Bates, and seven white males began singing together when a "whole bunch of Negroes suddenly jumped into the gondola, two of them shooting pistols and the others showing knives." According to Price, the black youths threw all but one of the white males from the train. After one of the black youths punched her in the mouth, she said, the Scottsboro Boys held knives to her and Bates and raped them.

As Price talked to the newsmen, Ruby Bates kept mum, nodding occasionally. Younger than Price, seventeen-year-old Ruby was quiet and insecure. Her timidity likely was the result of her rough childhood. Her father was a heavy drinker who had beaten his kids, and her mother was a prostitute. They lived in an unpainted shack in Huntsville, and Bates, besides working in a cotton mill, frequently had sold her body—a fact she did not reveal to reporters.

Orville Gilley, the white youth taken from the train, added his own details to Price's tale. The nineteen-year-old hobo told reporters that one of the Scottsboro Boys pulled a gun on him and another placed a knife to his ribs. It should be noted, however, that Gilley made his living reciting his own poetry in various towns, and seemed to relish the attention from the curious reporters.

The papers also reported a claim made by Roy Wright that the Chattanooga four were innocent—that the other five committed the crime. With Price's, Gilley's, and Wright's accusations trumpeted in the news-

Orville Gilley, a traveling poet, confirmed and embellished Victoria Price's testimony of what happened aboard the train. *(Courtesy of AP Images)*

papers, Jackson County's white residents were convinced of the Scottsboro Boys' guilt. Days after the incident, a grand jury quickly indicted them all, even the thirteen year olds. The trial for all nine was set to begin on April 6. Aware that the nation's skeptical eyes were upon them, spokesmen for the region promised a fair trial. Yet the *Jackson County Sentinel* assured readers of a conviction, stating that "the evidence against the negroes was so conclusive as to be almost perfect."

Before the trial could begin the Scottsboro Boys needed a lawyer. No one in the area was willing to represent them. Finally, Milo C. Moody, age sixty-nine, stepped forward. Moody had passed the bar in 1889 but had never completed college. Though he had been a respected attorney decades earlier, his abilities had eroded over time and he struggled to find work. He agreed to represent the Scottsboro Boys because it paid a modest fee.

Moody would be assisted by the even less reliable Stephen R. Roddy. Roddy signed on for $120 to serve as an "advisor," despite his lack of experience in criminal law. A well-known drinker, Roddy had been arrested in 1930 because of public drunkenness.

With Moody and Roddy representing them, and a white populace itching to convict, the Scottsboro Boys appeared doomed. The state of Alabama would ask for the death penalty—the electric chair—because black men's rape of white women was considered to be the ultimate crime.

According to Patterson, the Scottsboro Boys' attorneys never talked to them in the week preceding the trial. They got most of their information from white prisoners, who had read the newspapers and talked to the guards. "They told us, 'If you ever see a good chance, you better run,'" Patterson wrote. "They said they're going to give every one of you the death seat. . . . I couldn't believe that. I am an unbelieving sort."

three
Death Sentence

T he trial opened on the first Monday of the month. It was Fair Day in Scottsboro, when farmers from all over the region flocked into town to buy and trade goods, gossip, and sometimes attend trials at the courthouse. On this Fair Day whites came from miles around—by foot, horse-drawn wagon, and automobile—to witness perhaps the biggest event in Scottsboro history.

The crowd expanded to several thousand, only a small fraction of which would be allowed into the visitor's section of the courthouse. Armed guards, some with machine guns, surrounded the building and kept onlookers at bay. The atmosphere was more festive than hostile, although some in the crowd cursed at defense attorney Stephen Roddy as he worked his way through the crowd.

A nervous Roddy, alcohol on his breath, took a seat at the defense table, and Judge Alfred Hawkins called the courtroom to order at 9 a.m. When Hawkins asked Roddy if he

A large crowd gathered around the Scottsboro courthouse on the first day of the trial. *(Courtesy of AP Images)*

was representing the defendants, he replied, "Not exactly." He and Moody had spent less than a half-hour interviewing their clients.

Roddy requested a change of venue, claiming that jurors could not be unbiased due to the lynch-mob atmosphere in Scottsboro over the past week. However, Jackson County Sheriff M. L. Wann and National Guard Major Joseph Starnes claimed that the crowds had been just curious, not hostile. Judge Hawkins ruled that the trial would remain in the Scottsboro courtroom.

Circuit Solicitor H. G. Bailey, a tall, gray-haired, pleasant-looking man, decided to try the nine defendants in four separate trials, to be held in succession. Clarence Norris and

Charlie Weems would be tried first, followed by Haywood Patterson. Olen Montgomery, Ozie Powell, Willie Roberson, Eugene Williams, and Andy Wright would go on trial next, and thirteen-year-old Roy Wright would be tried last.

Despite what the U.S. Constitution stated, the Scottsboro Boys would not have a jury of their peers. White Southerners prevented nearly all blacks from registering to vote, and people could not serve on a jury unless they were registered to vote. Also, the all-white Jackson County jury commission selected the pool of jurors, and they were not about to choose any African Americans. By 2:30, the all-white jury was selected.

Victoria Price answers questions on the witness stand. *(Courtesy of Bettmann/Corbis)*

Prosecutor Bailey then called his first witness, Victoria Price, who took the stand wearing a new dress, full of vigor.

Prompted by prosecutor Bailey, Price mesmerized the courtroom with her version of the incident. According to Price, she and Bates were returning from Chattanooga on the morning of March 25 after a failed attempt to find employment in the cotton mills. After a while, the women joined seven white males in a gondola (an open freight car shaped like a shoe box). All was fine, she said, until twelve black youths jumped from an adjacent boxcar into the gondola.

Two of the African Americans waved pistols and every one of the twelve carried an open knife. They ordered the white males off the train. "All you sons of bitches unload," she claimed to have heard one say. Then the black youths hit one of the white boys on the head with a pistol.

At that point, according to Price, Clarence Norris confronted her. "Are you going to put out?" he demanded. When she said no, six of the defendants, she claimed, held her down and raped her in succession. One of them, she said, held a knife to her throat. She remembered each of the six: Norris, Weems, Patterson, Montgomery, and the Wrights. Price said that the ordeal seemed to last for hours. She resisted the entire time, she said, but was beaten and bruised by her attackers. Price said she put her clothes back on after the rape, but when she got off the train in Paint Rock she lost consciousness.

Price's testimony won over the jury, putting pressure on Roddy. During cross-examination, he tried to portray her as a woman of questionable character. He asked how many times she had been married, to which she replied twice. But when he asked if she had ever been in jail, Bailey objected and Judge Hawkins sustained. With no more questions, Price stepped down.

Bailey next questioned Dr. R. R. Bridges, who had examined Price and Bates shortly after she departed the train. Bridges testified that "Victoria Price was not hysterical at all," and that all he found on her body were some small bruises on her hips and some short scratches on her left arm. His examination revealed semen in the vaginas of both Price and Bates, but the sperm was nonmotile. (Motile, meaning self-propelled, sperm survive in the vagina from three to twenty-four hours. Nonmotile sperm can remain in the vagina from fourteen

Dr. R. R. Bridges examined Price and Bates soon after they disembarked from the train and made accusations of rape. In this photo, Judge Horton leans in to hear Dr. Bridges's testimony. *(Courtesy of AP Images)*

hours to seventeen days after intercourse.) Dr. Bridges did state that it was possible that she was raped. Dr. Marvin Lynch had also examined the women on March 25. He corroborated Dr. Bridge's testimony, but he added that they found only a trace of semen in the vagina of Victoria Price.

The trial resumed the next morning, with a smaller but still substantial crowd milling around the well-guarded courthouse. A nervous, hesitant Ruby Bates was the first witness of the day. Her account of the alleged rapes differed from Price's. For one thing, Bates said that she and Price had visited one cotton mill in Chattanooga, not multiple mills as her friend had claimed. Also, Bates stated that two black youths entered the gondola first, and then several others came aboard a few minutes later—much different than Price's claim of a dozen black males storming the gondola at once. However, Roddy did not press Bates to explain the discrepancies.

Prosecutor Bailey put five more witnesses on the stand, with farmer Luther Morris providing the most potent testimony. While he was standing in the loft of his barn, about thirty yards from railroad tracks, Morris claimed that he saw several black youths "put off five white men and take charge of two girls." Morris said that the white males immediately ran back toward Stevenson.

Bailey then rested his case. The defense attorneys' only witnesses were the defendants themselves. Charlie Weems admitted that a fight occurred on the train. He said that Haywood Patterson, who carried a pistol, hit one of the white boys and that the rest of the whites jumped off the train—except Gilley, whom the black youths prevented from jumping because the train was going too fast. Bailey tried to rattle Weems with rapid-fire questions, but Charlie stuck

Ruby Bates often appeared nervous and hesitant during her testimonies.
(Courtesy of AP Images)

to his story. Weems claimed that he had nothing to do with Price and Bates, and that the defendants never even shared the same car as the two women.

Clarence Norris was put on the stand next, and under cross-examination, Norris dropped a bombshell: He claimed that all of the accused except him were guilty. He insisted that Roy Wright had held a knife on one of the women, and that the other seven raped the women in succession. "They all raped her [Price]," he declared loudly, "every one of them."

Norris thought that he could save himself with his testimony, but he was sadly mistaken. With Roddy's case now completely in shambles, he asked Bailey to drop the death sentence for Weems and Norris in exchange for life imprisonment but Bailey declined. Then, after trying to get Norris to change his story under oath, Roddy rested the defense.

Following up, Bailey introduced a witness, Arthur Woodall, who stated that he had found a knife on Norris—which, Price said, Norris had stolen from her.

Roddy and Moody declined to make closing remarks to the jury, but Bailey and attorney John Snodgrass did address the dozen men who would decide Weems' and Norris' fates. Then, after hearing instructions from Judge Hawkins, the jury left to decide the case.

That afternoon, on Tuesday, April 7, Haywood Patterson's trial began in the same courtroom. Price testified again, this time implicating Patterson directly. He not only was one of the two defendants who carried a pistol, she testified, but he definitely had raped her. When Roddy inquired about whether she engaged in prostitution, Price replied that she had not had intercourse with any white man except her husbands.

After uneventful testimony by Bates, the bailiff told Judge Hawkins that the Weems-Norris jury had reached a decision. The Patterson jury left the room, and the initial jury entered. Weems and Norris nervously awaited their fate. The court clerk read the foreman's verdict: "We find the defendants guilty of rape and fix their sentence at death."

The courtroom erupted in applause. Judge Hawkins pounded his gavel, but to no avail. Word immediately swept the crowd outside, more than a thousand strong, and they too roared their approval. Only when National Guardsmen began removing spectators did the noise die down.

Roddy then made his smartest move yet, motioning for a mistrial for Patterson because his jury had heard—and were presumably influenced—by the cheering. Hawkins denied the motion, however, and Patterson's trial continued. A new witness, Ory Dobbins, claimed that when he saw the train pass, he viewed one of the black youths throwing down a woman.

When Patterson took the stand his testimony was full of contradictions. At first he said he saw five of the defendants rape Price, but then he stated that he never saw the women on the train. Young Roy Wright then added to the confusion when he claimed that he saw nine black youths having intercourse with Price and Bates—excluding himself, his brother, Williams, and Patterson. With that testimony, the eventful second day of the trials concluded.

On Wednesday, another excited crowd gathered around the courthouse as Patterson's trial continued. Inside, Andy Wright, Williams, and Powell all testified that they did not see any women in the gondola. Montgomery claimed that he sat alone on the train and was unaware of any commotion at all. Then the trial was over.

Late that morning, Patterson's jury began deliberations. Minutes later, Powell, Williams, Roberson, Montgomery, and Andy Wright went on trial. During her testimony in this trial, Price provided more details of the alleged rape, insisting that Williams, Montgomery, and Andy Wright had raped her. Powell and Roberson, she said emphatically, had raped her friend Ruby. Price also upped the number of gunshots that she had heard on the gondola—from the one or two she claimed in her previous testimony, to seven this time.

Before lunch, the current jury was dismissed and Patterson's jury entered the room. He too was found guilty of rape and sentenced to death. Years later, Patterson would write: "Within two hours the jury had come back with a conviction. I was convicted in their minds before I went on trial. . . . All that spoke for me on that witness stand was my black skin—which didn't do so good."

When testimony resumed for Powell and the other four, Bates stated that she had been raped by six black men. Unlike Price, she could not remember any of them. When Dr. Bridges took the stand, the defense asked how Roberson could possibly have had intercourse since he suffered badly from gonorrhea and syphilis. Bridges said the act would have been painful for Roberson but possible.

All five of the defendants took the stand. Roberson said that when on the train his genitals were sore and swollen. Montgomery, with partial vision in one eye and none in the other, said his eyesight was too poor to recognize anyone from the train. Powell, Wright, and Williams denied having any interaction at all with the women on the train. But Price, back on the stand again, declared that both Weems and Williams held a knife to her throat while she was raped.

Orville Gilley, a witness for the first time, stated that he saw all five defendants in the gondola. After closing arguments, the jury left to deliberate.

On Wednesday, Roy Wright was the last of the Scottsboro Boys to be tried, and his trial ended that same day. Due to Wright's age, thirteen, Solicitor Bailey asked for life imprisonment instead of death. By late that evening, juries for the third and fourth trials had not yet reached a decision.

On Thursday morning, the jury for the five defendants declared each of them guilty and assigned the penalty of death. With Roy Wright's jury still undecided, Judge Hawkins ordered they be polled in open court. Some of the jurors agreed with Bailey's recommendation of life imprisonment, but most voted for death for the young teen. With the jury deadlocked, Hawkins declared a mistrial, which meant Roy Wright would have to be tried again.

Late that afternoon, Judge Hawkins addressed all of the defendants except Roy Wright. With eyes damp with tears, the judge declared: "It is the judgment of the court and the sentence of the law that the defendants be sentenced to death by electrocution at Kilby Prison in the City of Montgomery, Montgomery County, Alabama, on Friday the 10th day of July, 1931."

Normally in the Jim Crow South, the judge's ruling would have been the final word. The rapists would spend the rest of their doomed lives on death row. But this case—complete with its shocking accusations, questionable evidence, large number of defendants, and the young ages of the accused— had spurred national interest. African American groups demanded that each case be appealed, as did another organization with a strong political agenda. Shortly after sentencing, the International Labor Defense of the American Communist Party sent a duplicate telegram to Judge Hawkins and Alabama governor Ben Miller. "We demand stay of execution," the telegram stated, "and opportunity to investigate and prepare for new trial or appeal."

The juries had thought they had imposed typical Jim Crow justice on the Scottsboro Boys, but the case was far from over. In fact, it had barely begun.

four
Communist Influence

During the first decades of the twentieth century, the political and economic philosophy of communism gained favor among some intellectuals and labor leaders in Europe and the United States. Communists thought that an equitable and just society could not develop as long as a tiny minority of people controlled most of the wealth and the means of production. An economic system divided between the owners of the factories that produced the world's goods, and the vast majority of those who had no choice but to spend their lives working in the factories—those whose only capital was their labor—would inevitably lead a tyranny of the rich over the masses of poor.

Those who believed in communism struggled for decades to seize control of a nation, and to alter its system from capitalism to communism. Finally, in the midst of the suffering of World War I, a small dedicated group of Communist revolutionaries—the Bolsheviks—seized power in Russia. Over the next decades the Bolsheviks set out to create the Communist ideal of a classless society.

The dream of a classless society appealed to many in the United States, and the attraction of communism grew more appealing after the stock market crash of 1929 and the ensuing Great Depression that devastated the economy and left millions unemployed during the 1930s. The Communist Party of the USA, also known as the Communist Party USA or CPUSA, operated under the slogan "the united front from below."

The CPUSA worked to attract members regardless of race, and the injustices of racism and racial segregation created ample opportunities to attract African Americans. The CPUSA developed social and charitable organizations, such as the Harlem Unemployment Council in New York City, to get their message into the African American community. Another CPUSA organization, the International Labor Defense (ILD), was established to protest racial discrimination, police brutality, and lynching, and in some cases the ILD provided free legal counsel to black defendants.

The case of the Scottsboro Boys was a perfect opportunity for the ILD to win the hearts of the nation's African Americans on a national stage. In April, the ILD sent attorneys Joseph Brodsky and Allan Taub to Kilby Prison, where they met with the Scottsboro Boys and assured them that the cases would be appealed.

It was welcoming news to the nine inmates, who were already succumbing to the hell of prison life. Their first night at Kilby, they had shown their anger by ripping up their bedding and throwing food through the bars. The guards responded with fury. "They beat on us with their fists," claimed Patterson, "they kicked and tramped on our legs. The sheriff said to me: 'see that gallows, nigger. If you don't quieten' down I'll take you around to that gallows and hang you myself.'"

Regardless of whether the ILD lawyers actually cared for their defendants, or if their objective was purely political, they took strong action. On April 18, 1931, they informed the Chattanooga Negro Ministers' Alliance that they would represent the defendants for free, although they would need help with fund-raising. Attorney George W. Chamlee was hired to head the case. A small, eccentric man, Chamlee

Communists rally in support of the Scottsboro Boys in this 1933 picture. *(Courtesy of AP Images)*

convinced the Scottsboro Boys to sign an affidavit turning their defense over to the ILD.

The Communists were not the only ones who wanted to represent the Boys. NAACP officials, under the leadership of Walter White, also believed their organization should be fighting on behalf of the young black males, and to attract them away from the Communists. Dr. P. A. Stephens, of both the NAACP and the Chattanooga Negro Ministers' Alliance, ventured into Kilby Prison and had the nine inmates sign a statement cutting their ties with the ILD.

However, the ILD refused to back down. This began a bitter conflict between the ILD and the NAACP. According to Clarence Norris, both the ILD and NAACP sent money to the Boys— three dollars a month from the NAACP and eight dollars monthly from the ILD.

The Communists attacked the NAACP as a weak organization that kowtowed to the white establishment. The *Daily Worker,* a New York-based Communist newspaper, stated that the NAACP "will kiss the rope that hangs their brothers, if only the rope is blessed by a ruling class judge."

As a group, the NAACP was opposed to communism. Furthermore, there was the ever present fear that the white majority would obliterate their organization if they thought it was allied with Communists, or if it engaged in militant or confrontational behavior. They thought that if the Boys aligned themselves with ILD it would mean almost certain death.

ILD officials were so determined to represent the Scottsboro Boys that they even wowed their parents. They convinced the fathers and the mothers to write letters and visit Kilby in order to sway their children to let the ILD defend them.

Walter White, executive secretary of the NAACP, believed the NAACP could provide better legal defense for the Scottsboro Boys than the Communist-led ILD. *(Library of Congress)*

At a Communist rally in New York City, Janie Patterson—Haywood's mother—spoke on behalf of her son. A *New York Times* headlined explained what happened next: "Police Clubs Rout 200 Defiant Reds; Smash Banners and Scatter Harlem Marchers Who Lacked Permit."

Meanwhile, Communist groups throughout Europe used the Scottsboro case as inflammatory anti-American propaganda. In Dresden, Germany, young Communists flung bottles through the windows of the American consulate. Inside the bottles were notes that read: "Down with American murder and Imperialism. For the brotherhood of black and white young proletarians. An end to the bloody lynching of our Negro co-workers." Similar protests broke out in other European cities.

Back in Kilby Prison, the Scottsboro Boys could not decide who they wanted to represent them. Some picked the ILD, some the NAACP, and the argument went back and forth. Judge Hawkins had set June 5, 1931, to hear arguments regarding the motions for new trials. The hearing would be held in Fort Payne, Alabama. At the hearing, Brodsky and Chamlee arrived on behalf of the ILD; Stephen Roddy and Roderick Beddow—an attorney from Birmingham, Alabama—showed up representing the NAACP. Judge Hawkins declared that the defendants needed to agree on their attorneys, but in the meantime all the lawyers in the courtroom were allowed to make their arguments.

Both sets of lawyers argued that the defendants had been denied due process, as guaranteed by the Fourteenth Amendment, because the large, one-sided crowds had influenced the juries. In addition, the ILD attorneys submitted signed statements from black residents of Chattanooga that claimed that Victoria Price and Ruby Bates often prostituted themselves with black men in their community. Oliver Love, who ran a black boardinghouse, stated that he had allowed Price to use a room in his house on a regular basis for prostitution. Reports gathered by the American Civil Liberties Union and the Commission on Interracial Cooperation confirmed the women's prostitution.

The claims that she was a prostitute contradicted Price's testimony, in which she said she did not have sex outside of her marriage. Nevertheless, the locals were furious that the Communist lawyers had made such "attacks" on the two Southern women.

After the hearing, the fight over who would represent the Scottsboro Boys heated up, with both sides trying to sway the parents. In early June, William Pickens of the NAACP arrived at the home of Eugene Williams' mother where he found "one of the reds leading the Patterson couple like two dumb animals, jumping them into his car and racing off to some place where the Williams woman had already been concealed to prevent any intelligence from reaching her."

The defendants continued to vacillate as to which side they should join. Then, in late May, Ozzie Powell, Charlie Weems, and Clarence Norris committed to the NAACP, and the rest went with the ILD.

On June 22, 1931, Judge Hawkins set aside the July 10 execution date. Another black man, Willie Stokes, was electrocuted instead that day. After hearing the grisly details of his execution, many of the Boys suffered nightmares and restless nights.

Later that summer, with most of the Boys firmly in the ILD camp, Walter White of the NAACP played a trump card—he

At the time Clarence Darrow agreed to represent the Scottsboro Boys, he was one of the most respected and well-known lawyers in the U.S. *(Library of Congress)*

convinced Clarence Darrow to take on the case. Darrow, the most revered trial lawyer in America, had risen to fame by defending the underdog, including minorities. In 1925, he had won acquittal for African American Henry Sweet, who had shot and killed a member of a white mob.

Nevertheless, the Communists were so dogged and persuasive that none of the Scottsboro Boys moved to Darrow and the NAACP. In fact, by early December, Powell, Weems, and Norris had changed their minds and moved into the ILD's camp.

Three days after Christmas, at the urging of Darrow, attorneys for both organizations met to settle the situation. Brodsky and Chamlee represented the ILD at the meeting; Darrow, Beddow, and Arthur Hays were there for the NAACP. They debated for hours. Brodsky and Chamlee said they did not want to be involved with the NAACP, which the CPUSA had frequently condemned. Conversely, the NAACP trio did not want to be associated with the Communists. They argued that having Communist representation would hinder the Boys as they moved through the American justice system.

Finally, Darrow made a proposal. The five attorneys in the room would represent the Boys, he suggested, with no formal ties to the ILD and NAACP. Chamlee took that offer back to George Maurer, his boss in New York. Maurer countered that Darrow and Hays should publicly resign as NAACP attorneys and sign on as ILD attorneys and abide by all ILD decisions. For Darrow and Hays, this was out of the question. On January 4, 1932, the NAACP decided to formally withdraw from the case.

Beginning on January 21, 1932, the ILD attorneys would present their case to the Alabama Supreme Court.

five

All the Way to the Supreme Court

One of the things many white Southerners raged about during the Jim Crow era was "outside agitators" who came into the South and tried to end segregation. Righteous Northerners, black activists, and especially New York-based Communists, whom Southerners claimed were out to destroy the "southern way" of life, infuriated them. On January 21, 1932, when ILD attorneys Joseph Brodsky and George Chamlee appeared before the Alabama Supreme Court, the justices greeted them with cold, burning stares, visibly seething with anger.

After the ILD got involved in the Scottsboro case in the spring of 1931, Communists and black Alabamians began to work more closely together. Several black men formed the Alabama Share Croppers Union and made a list of demands from landlords, including the continuation of food advances, the right of sharecroppers to market their own crops, and a minimum wage of $1 a day. They also demanded freedom for the Scottsboro Boys.

Alabama's political establishment had no intention of tolerating a Communist-inspired union of black workers. On July 15, 1931, police raided a secret union meeting in Camp Hill, Alabama, instigating a shootout between the police and union members. Union leader Ralph Gray was killed, and more than forty people were arrested—several African Americans were lynched.

In August 1931, the murder of two white women—Jennie Wood and Augusta Williams—by a black man in Birmingham set off a frenzy of violence. Whites bombed a black barbershop, shot at African Americans on the streets, and did house-to-house searches. When some of the searches uncovered leftist literature, The *Birmingham News* blamed the trouble on Communist agitation: "If this is one of the outgrowths of communism on these shores; if this is the aim of the propaganda of that doctrine, then Southerners and all Americans . . . who understand the inequalities of the races . . . must by every possible means lance out of the social body these infamous and unnatural teachings."

Anxieties in Birmingham reached the point of hysteria when Augusta Williams' sister, Nell Williams, claimed she recognized the man who killed Augusta. Originally, Nell had described the killer as a stocky man with a mustache and dark skin. But the African American whom she eventually identified as the killer, Willie Peterson, was thin with lighter skin, and had never worn a mustache. Moreover, witnesses swore that he had been on the other side of town when the murders had occurred.

While Peterson was in custody, Nell's brother, Dent Williams, shot him three times, but he survived. Although the state officials knew Peterson was innocent, they prosecuted him anyway and he was found guilty and sentenced to death. The governor later commuted the sentence to life in prison. Clearly, the word of a white woman, regardless of its validity, was enough to send an innocent black man to death row.

As the NAACP had warned, the agitation of the Communists was creating a backlash, but they didn't seem to care. The lawyers of the ILD wanted to use the case to help foment a workers' revolution, their ultimate goal. In their New York offices, *Daily Worker* writers banged out scathing copy against Alabama's white establishment. In one edition, the *Daily Worker* instructed: "Negro and white workers, smash this murderous frame-up. Hold protest meetings. Wire protests to the governor of Alabama." The newspaper also declared that the Scottsboro Boys were innocent "victims of a murderous frame up concocted by the Alabama bosses and their state and court machinery."

As the Alabama Supreme Court justices began hearings for the appeal on January 21, 1932, an enraged Chief Justice John C. Anderson announced that the court had received numerous threats. "These messages are highly improper, inflammatory, and revolutionary in nature," he told Chamlee and Brodsky, and they were "sent with the evident intent to bulldoze this court."

Chamlee replied that the ILD had nothing to do with the threatening messages, but the justices didn't believe it. Clearly, if the ILD attorneys were going to win the appeal in this hostile courtroom, they had a lot of work to do.

SMASH the SCOTTSBORO LYNCH VERDICT

By JAMES S. ALLEN

1c

This image appears on the front cover of a pamphlet produced by the ILD.
(Courtesy of the Michigan State University Library, Special Collections Division)

A button distributed by the ILD *(Courtesy of the David J. & Janice L. Frent Collection/Corbis)*

Brodsky, who presented most of the arguments in court, stated several reasons why the trials of the eight defendants had been improper. First, because Alabama juries did not include African Americans, the defendants did not get a jury of their peers, as guaranteed in the U.S. Constitution. Secondly, he noted that thirteen-year-old Roy Wright, by law, should have been tried in a juvenile court. Finally, Brodsky argued that the jury could not possibly have been impartial due to the biased commentary from the local newspapers and the large, white crowds that swarmed the courthouse.

Chamlee followed Brodsky and argued that the defendants had not received proper counsel. In fact, they had not even been permitted to consult with a lawyer before the day that the trial began. Chamlee also pointed out that attorney Stephen Roddy had stated on the record that he had not been hired to represent the defendants.

The next day, Thomas Knight Jr., presented arguments for the state. Knight was Alabama's attorney general—and the son of one of the justices on the state's Supreme Court. Knight did little to refute most of the defense attorneys' claims. It was not surprising that the jury was influenced by the angry mobs, he said, for it was the natural Southerners' passion for protecting white womanhood.

In reality, Knight didn't need to speak at all. Despite the arguments of the defense, and the strong evidence that the Scottsboro Boys did not receive a fair trial, on March 24 the Alabama Supreme Court upheld the convictions. This came as no surprise. The court did grant Eugene Williams a new trial because he was a juvenile—only thirteen years old—during his first trial.

In his decision, Thomas Knight Sr., Alabama Supreme Court justice and father of the prosecutor, addressed the defense's major claims. He found that the hundred militiamen at the courthouse didn't influence the jury but instead assured those in the courtroom that the state would conduct lawful trials. Also, the swift justice of the trials (eight death-penalty convictions within fifteen days of the alleged crime) was not unduly hasty. To the contrary, it was a protection of the defendants' constitutional right to a speedy trial. Knight also dismissed the defense's claim that they had not been tried before a jury of their peers. The state had the right to fix the qualifications for jurors, within constitutional limitations, and the Scottsboro Boys had been tried according to those rights. Knight finished up by setting new dates for the execution of the seven condemned Scottsboro Boys.

Reactions to the ruling were predictable; to southern whites, the court's decision legitimized the initial verdicts; for opponents of Jim Crow it was additional proof of state-sanctioned injustice in the Deep South.

Despite the court's ruling, the Scottsboro Boys still had reason to hope. The ILD hired Walter Pollak, a prominent constitutional attorney, to appeal the case to the United States Supreme Court. On May 27, Pollak presented initial arguments to the high court. His goal in the initial arguments was to convince the justices of the Supreme Court to review the case. In order to do that he had to convince them that an

The U.S. Supreme Court building *(Library of Congress)*

issue concerning the U.S. Constitution was involved. On May 27, 1932, the U.S. Supreme Court agreed to hear the case.

On October 10, 1932, Pollak presented the Scottsboro Boy's case to the U.S. Supreme Court in the case of *Powell v. Alabama*. He stressed the same points that Brodsky and Chamlee had presented in the Alabama Supreme Court, but gave extra emphasis to the mistakes that were made in jury selection. He pointed out that although the population of Jackson County, Alabama, was predominantly African American, no black citizens had served on a Jackson County jury since the days of Reconstruction.

As the Supreme Court justices considered the case, they focused on the Sixth and Fourteenth Amendments to the U.S. Constitution:

> **Sixth Amendment:** In all criminal prosecutions, the accused shall enjoy the right to a speedy and public trial, by an impartial jury of the State and district wherein the crime shall have been committed, which district shall have been previously ascertained by law, and to be informed of the nature and cause of the accusation; to be confronted with the witnesses against him; to have compulsory process for obtaining witnesses in his favor, and to have the Assistance of Counsel for his defense.

> **Fourteenth Amendment:** No State shall make or enforce any law which shall abridge the privileges or immunities of citizens of the United States; nor shall any State deprive any person of life, liberty, or property, without due process of law; nor deny to any person within its jurisdiction the equal protection of the laws.

On November 7, amid protests and arrests outside the Supreme Court building, Justice George Sutherland announced the court's decision. By a margin of 7-2, the court voted in favor of the Scottsboro Boys. The court agreed that the Boys had been denied due process because of the exclusion of African Americans from the jury.

However, the justices devoted more attention to another issue. They decided that the defendants had been denied effective counsel. Sutherland stated that during arraignment the defendants had not been asked if they had or were able to employ counsel or if they had wished to have counsel appointed to them. Judge Hawkins had assigned all seven members of the local bar to represent the Boys, but the "all call" wasn't good enough, according to the high court—particularly when all seven local lawyers refused to represent them.

Sutherland further noted that defendants should have an opportunity to obtain counsel of their own choice. The Scottsboro Boys did not have that opportunity. Milo Moody and Stephen Roddy were essentially foisted upon them. Moreover, no attorney was officially assigned to represent the defendants until the morning of the trial, which began at 9 a.m. Wrote Sutherland: "Under the circumstances disclosed, we hold that defendants were not accorded the right of counsel in any substantial sense. To decide otherwise would simply be to ignore actualities."

Powell v. *Alabama* turned out to be a landmark case in the struggle for civil rights in the U.S. because the Supreme Court ruled that in a capital trial defendants must be given access to counsel upon their request. Defendants are as much entitled to "Assistance of Counsel" while preparing for trial as during the trial itself. It was unclear whether the court's decision applied to non-capital trials as well. However, the court's ruling went a long way in strengthening the rights of

Haywood Patterson sits in prison after receiving the death sentence.
(Courtesy of AP Images)

future defendants who were too poor to afford their own attorney. For the Scottsboro Boys, the decision offered fresh hope. Wrote Patterson: "On November 8, 1932, the boys shouted, they were so glad. Andy Wright, from his cell, read out loud that we fellows won a new trial."

The new trials were scheduled for March 1933, and more good news followed. Judge Hawkins approved the ILD's request for a change of venue, and in early January the ILD found exciting new evidence. They discovered a letter purportedly signed by Ruby Bates, seemingly exonerating the defendants.

In a letter addressed to a man named "Earl," Bates wrote that it was a "lie about those Negroes jassing me" and that "those police man made me tell a lie." She added that "those Negroes did not touch me," "i was drunk at the time and did not know what i was doing," and "i Wish those Negroes are not Burnt on account of me."

Unfortunately for the Boys, circumstances surrounding the letter undercut its value as evidence. Police in Huntsville, Alabama, found the letter in the possession of Miron Pearlman, a former boxer, after they arrested him for drunkenness. Questioned by police, Pearlman said that attorney George Chamlee had paid him to get Bates drunk and have her write a letter saying that the black youths had not raped her.

Bates quickly signed an affidavit in which she supported Pearlman's statement. She swore: "I was drunk last night and have no recollection of writing any letter. That the letter supposed to have written by me to [Earl] Streetman contains all falsehoods, no truth being in it, and I deny making any such statements or writing any such letter."

This turn of events could have put Chamlee in danger of being disbarred for bribery, but there was a lack of evidence, indicating that the forgery charges were untrue. However, the letter could not be used by the defense in future cases.

As they waited for their new trials to begin, the Scottsboro Boys continued to endure life in Kilby Prison. Not only were they on death row, but the "guards hated us because of all the attention we got from outside world," Clarence Norris wrote. "They came into our cells and abused us at will." When Norris complained of a toothache the guards pinned him down in his cell while a dentist yanked out a different tooth.

In early March 1933, they were transferred to the jail in Decatur, Alabama, where the new trials would be held. As hard as it was for them to believe, their new home would turn out to be even more horrific than Kilby. The March 27 trial date couldn't come fast enough.

six

Judge Horton's Skepticism

After the change of venue was granted the ILD lawyers hoped the new trials would be held in Birmingham. Even though the juries would still be all-white, Birmingham was a much larger city and the citizenry were better educated and—the defense hoped—would be a little less bigoted.

However, Decatur, Alabama, was named as the new venue. Located fifty miles west of Scottsboro, Decatur had a population of about 15,000, and, although larger, had a mind-set similar to that in Scottsboro. The Decatur jail was in such shambles that it had been deemed unfit for white prisoners—but was acceptable to house black citizens. Recalled Norris, "It was filthy, dust everywhere, big holes were in the floors and walls, plaster fell down around our heads, the stink was sickening and rats the size of rabbits had the run of the place. But the bedbugs! There were millions of them."

Samuel Leibowitz meets with the Scottsboro Boys in prison. *(Courtesy of Bettmann/Corbis)*

If nothing else, the defendants could at least be grateful for their new attorney, who joined the team of George Chamlee and Joseph Brodsky. The ILD was excited to land Samuel Leibowitz, who replaced the recently retired Clarence Darrow as one of the leading criminal defense lawyers in America. "Your organization and I are not in agreement in our political and economic views," Liebowitz wrote to the ILD, but he agreed to take the case to defend "the basic rights of man."

Leibowitz, a balding, Jewish New Yorker, knew he would be treated as an outcast in the Decatur courthouse. In his comments to reporters before the trial he tried to distance himself from the Communist ILD and to laud the citizens of Alabama. His opponent in the courtroom would be Thomas Knight, the well-connected, energetic attorney general for Alabama. Liebowitz knew he was a better lawyer and that he had a stronger case, but he also knew that he was still the underdog because of Knight's tremendous "home-court" advantage.

At least this time there was a relatively level-headed judge presiding over the case. The soft-spoken James Horton was about as fair as they came in Alabama. Still, it was abundantly clear that Leibowitz was fighting an uphill battle; the hostility toward the defendants and their attorneys was so hot the National Guard was called in to patrol the town.

Haywood Patterson was the first of the Scottsboro Boys to be retried. The defense opened with a motion to overturn the 1931 convictions since no African Americans had been on the jury rolls in Jackson County, but Judge Horton overruled the motion.

When Victoria Price took the stand as the first witness, Knight pulled a torn pair of women's underwear from his briefcase and asked Price if they were hers. When Leibowitz objected to this tactic by saying women's underwear hadn't been shown in any court in two years, Knight tossed them toward the jury and said, "Well, they're here now." The courtroom erupted in laughter.

In his cross-examination of Victoria Price, Liebowitz displayed a toy replica of the train, custom-made by the Lionel Corporation. When he questioned Price about where she was on the train, and asked her about her checkered past, she was uncharacteristically tight-lipped. Dr. R. R. Bridges also testified on Monday. He reiterated his earlier testimony

When Liebowitz used this toy replica of the freight train in the courtroom to question Price, she became flustered and silent. *(Courtesy of AP Images)*

that Price and Bates had not shown signs of physical abuse or emotional damage when he examined them, but that he did believe the rapes had occurred.

The next day Dr. Marvin Lynch, the other doctor who had examined the alleged victims, was supposed to testify for the state. Knight asked that Lynch be excused, and Judge Horton agreed, but then Lynch requested a private conversation with Horton.

Lynch told Horton that he was convinced the women were not sexually assaulted. "Judge," he said, "I looked at both the women and told them they were lying, that they knew they had not been raped, and they just laughed at me." Lynch told Horton that he didn't want to testify because if he sided with the black youths, "I'd never be able to go back into Jackson County."

When Judge Horton, who could not force Lynch to testify because he had already excused him, returned to the bench he appeared to be calm on the surface but also deeply troubled. As the state sent a parade of witnesses to the stand, the judge seemed to become increasingly doubtful that the rapes had occurred. When Ory Dobbins, the farmer who said he had witnessed the attacks as the train passed, swore that he saw a black male grab a woman in the gondola and throw her down, for example, he insisted she wore a dress, which was inaccurate. Both Price and Bates had worn men's overalls and women's coats.

Arthur H. Woodall, a part-time Jackson County deputy sheriff, presented powerful evidence for the state when he testified that he had found a small pen knife that Price later claimed was hers on one of the defendants shortly after he was arrested. According to Woodall, he could not remember which defendant had the knife, but that he had "said he took it off the white girl Victoria Price."

Woodall's testimony elicited such a stunned reaction from Liebowitz that Knight burst into laughter and ran out of the courtroom. Liebowitz demanded a mistrial because of Knight's action, but Horton denied it.

By Tuesday night the situation in the town was becoming ominous. Approximately two hundred people, irate about how Liebowitz had addressed Price and other witnesses, gathered in a near mob to "discuss" the matter. Several of them talked openly about lynching the Scottsboro Boys.

The following day, without the jury present, Horton lectured those in the courtroom. "I am speaking with feeling, and I know it, because I am feeling it," he said. Nearly shouting, he declared, "I absolutely have no patience with mob spirit." After more harsh words, he called for the jury so that Patterson's trial could resume.

On Wednesday afternoon, Knight questioned witnesses Andy Wright, Eugene Williams, and Patterson. All swore that they had never seen Price or Bates until the train stopped in Paint Rock. The attorney general tried to rattle Patterson by shouting questions, pacing furiously, and shaking his finger in his face, but Patterson did not break or divert from his testimony.

When it came time for Liebowitz to present the defense, his case picked up steam. Dr. Edward A. Reisman, a gynecologist from Chattanooga, testified that if a woman had been raped by six men it was inconceivable for her to have only a trace of semen in her vagina, which had been the case when Price was examined. He also said that sperm remain motile six to eight hours in a healthy vagina, but the sperm in Price's sample were nonmotile even though she had been examined just ninety minutes after the alleged rape.

In his testimony, Lester Carter, a friend of Price, explained the discrepancy. He said that on the night of March 23— two days before the alleged rape—he had intercourse with Ruby Bates and that Price had sex with her boyfriend, Jack Tiller.

Carter, who rode the train with Bates and Price, offered even more damning testimony. He said that in Scottsboro on March 25, several hours after the arrests, Price met with some of the white boys on the train. According to Carter, Price said that one of the boys needed to pretend to be her brother or else she could be arrested. This may have been in order to avoid arrest under the Mann Act, which prohibited crossing state lines for the purpose of prostitution or other practices deemed immoral. Later, Price asked Orville Gilley to support her story about being raped. "Gilley," said Carter, "told her to go to Hell. He didn't care for that."

In cross-examination, Morgan County Solicitor Wade Wright insisted that Carter had been bribed by the ILD lawyers to lie on the stand. Wright did get Carter to admit that defense attorney Joseph Brodsky had paid Carter's rent and bought him a new suit.

On Thursday, Leibowitz rested the defense, with the right to reopen it. Minutes later, as orchestrated by Leibowitz, his star witness dramatically entered the courtroom. Ruby Bates, chaperoned by a social worker from Birmingham, took the witness stand and under oath confirmed that she and Price had had sex with Carter and Tiller, respectively, on March 23, 1931. More importantly, she said that she was not aware of Price being raped on the train, and that she had been with

Price the entire time. Bates stated that while she lived in New York, a minister named Dr. Harry Emerson Fostick advised her to return to Alabama and speak the truth.

On cross-examination, prosecutor Knight worked to rip Bates's testimony to shreds. He pressured her about the letter found on Miron Pearlman and she responded that she did not know what she had written. As with Carter, the state insisted that Bates had been bribed. "Where did you get that coat?" Knight prodded. "Where did you get that hat . . . Who gave you the money to buy it?" Bates, in a whisper, replied, "Dr. Fostick of New York."

After Bates's testimony, each side prepared for final arguments. The local citizens were more hostile than ever toward the defense, whom they believed had bribed the witnesses. There was anxiety about what would happen if the Scottsboro Boys were found not guilty.

In his summation, Solicitor Wright prodded the jury to "show them that Alabama justice cannot be bought and sold with Jew money from New York." The remarks clearly roused the jury, while Leibowitz—slamming his hand on his table—demanded a mistrial because of the racial and inflammatory remarks. When it was his turn to speak to the jury, Leibowitz also delivered passionate closing remarks.

On Saturday, while instructing the jury, Horton told them to stick to the facts of the case. He even reiterated some of the important points that supported the defense, such as how evidence had shown that Price had made false statements. The jury, he said, was to decide whether Haywood Patterson was guilty of rape beyond a reasonable doubt.

On Sunday, Patterson—the only black person amid a sea of whites—awaited the verdict. Then Horton read the jury's

Pictured here is the all-white jury that tried the Scottsboro Boys in Decatur. *(Courtesy of AP Images)*

decision: "We find the defendant guilty as charged and fix the punishment at death in the electric chair." The twelve-member jury had voted that Patterson was guilty within five minutes of convening. Eleven immediately wanted the death penalty, while the foreman held out for life in prison for twelve hours before finally giving in.

The news of the verdict elicited celebration throughout the South and outrage in much of the North. In Harlem, outside the *Amsterdam News,* 20,000 African Americans signed a petition agreeing to participate in a protest march in Washington, D.C. When Liebowitz arrived via train in

New York, several thousand black citizens greeted him at Pennsylvania Station. Addressing the crowd, he spewed hatred for the enemy down South. "If you ever saw those creatures, those bigots whose mouths are slits in their faces, whose eyes popped out like frogs, whose chins drip tobacco juice, bewhiskered and filthy, you would not ask how they could do it."

On April 18, Judge Horton sentenced Patterson to die in the electric chair at Kilby Prison on June 16, then immediately suspended the sentence due to Brodsky's motion for a new trial. Horton also postponed the trials of the other Scottsboro Boys until passions in the area had died down.

On the weekend of May 6-7, William L. Patterson, executive secretary of the ILD, led several thousand protestors to Washington, D.C. Accompanied by Ruby Bates, Patterson asked to see President Franklin Roosevelt. Denied a meeting,

Protesters march through Washington, D.C., to petition President Roosevelt to free the Scottsboro Boys. *(Courtesy of AP Images)*

they then marched to the U.S. Capitol. Though Vice-President John Nance Garner and Speaker of the House Henry T. Rainey did talk to representatives of the marchers, Rainey insisted that the case was a matter for the courts, not Congress.

In the aftermath of the Patterson trial, many Southerners with more moderate views were conflicted about the verdict. The *Birmingham Post* announced that Patterson never should have been convicted because there was obvious reasonable doubt of his guilt. Meanwhile, Alabamians cracked down on "free thinkers" in their state. A black teacher who demanded the release of the Scottsboro Boys was not rehired, a rabbi who was vocal about the case was forced to resign, and a white woman who endorsed the ILD was jailed for fifty-three days.

On June 22, 1933, Judge Horton convened court to hear the defense's motion for a new trial. ILD attorneys Chamlee and Osmund K. Fraenkel thought they would have a fight on their hands, but they received a pleasant surprise. The judge opened with a long discourse, explaining why he thought that Price had fabricated her story.

Horton wondered why none of the white boys were called as witnesses to corroborate her story. Also, Price said that a defendant had cut her head with the butt of a pistol, but the doctors had not found any cuts or bruises. Nor did the doctors find her in a heightened emotional state. The judge wondered that after six rapes why no trace of semen was found on the skin of the defendants. Finally, why was only a tiny trace of semen found in the vagina of Price—and why was it nonmotile after only ninety minutes?

Said Horton, "[T]he conclusion becomes clear and clearer that this woman was not forced into intercourse with all of these Negroes upon that train, but that her condition was clearly due to the intercourse she had had on the nights previous to this time." The judge declared that he was setting aside the jury's verdict and the court's sentence, and that Haywood Patterson would be granted a new trial.

Horton, who had been lauded throughout Alabama immediately after the trial and the guilty verdicts, now was vilified by the state's newspapers and public officials. He was pressured to remove himself from the upcoming round of trials for the other Scottsboro Boys, scheduled for November 1933. When Horton campaigned for reelection in early 1934, he could not find political figures to support him and lost in the primary election. Meanwhile, Thomas K. Knight Jr., prosecutor of the Scottsboro Boys, was elected lieutenant governor.

Seven
Bigotry on the Bench

The state of Alabama wanted to retry the Scottsboro Boys quickly—and to make sure that the judge presiding would see that they were convicted again. They assigned Judge William Callahan to the case and it looked like they had found their man. Clarence Norris wrote that, "This judge was a redneck from the word go." Haywood Patterson added, "He couldn't get us to the chair fast enough."

Seventy years old, Callahan had never attended either college or law school, but had apprenticed in a Decatur, Alabama law office. He was exasperated by the case and tired of the national spotlight shining on his town, and wanted to process the trials as quickly as possible. He imposed strict limitations on media access, including the barring of photographers, and persuaded the governor not to employ the National Guard, which left the defense attorneys unprotected and at severe risk. In 1933, two ILD lawyers had been shot to death by a vigilante "firing squad" outside Tuscaloosa, Alabama for representing black defendants.

When the new trials began on November 20, 1933, it did not take long for Callahan to reveal his bigotry. Defense attorney Samuel Leibowitz opened with a motion for a change of venue, which the judge dismissed.

In another motion, Leibowitz urged that earlier indictments of the defendants be negated since African Americans were

John Vreeland Harding, a handwriting expert, testified that the Jackson County jury lists were tampered with. *(Courtesy of AP Images)*

deliberately excluded by Jackson County jury commission-
ers. To prove it, Leibowitz brought in J. E. Moody, head of
the Jackson County jury commission. Moody read the names
and race of those on the jury lists. For well over an hour,
Moody and then clerk C. A. Wann named one white person
after the other. Eventually, Wann came to the name of Hugh
Sanford—a black man. It turned out that at least ten African
Americans were on the list, but Leibowitz was convinced the
names were added at a later date. The next day, handwriting expert John Vreeland Harding testified that he believed
the lists had been tampered with, but Callahan rejected the
evidence of fraud and denied the motion to negate the 1931
indictments because of the all-white jury.

On Monday, November 24, as attorneys questioned potential jurors for the Patterson trial, Callahan cut Leibowitz
short and told him to speed it up. This sort of interference
in the defense's case became the norm during the attorney's
examination of witnesses. When Leibowitz caught a pan-
icking Victoria Price in a web of contradictions, the judge
frequently interrupted with comments such as, "Let's don't
take up time on that." "Speedy" Callahan, as reporters began
calling him, used his reprimands on the defense counsel and
allowed prosecutor Thomas Knight a free rein.

Leibowitz had hoped to call Ruby Bates as a witness, but
she was ill and was in a New York hospital, and Callahan
would not delay the trials until she was able to testify. Nor
would the judge allow Leibowitz to mention that Price had
intercourse with Jack Tiller on March 23, which would have
explained the semen in her vagina. According to Callahan,
this happened before the alleged crime and therefore wasn't
relevant.

During the closing arguments for the Patterson trial, the state tried to deflect attention from the facts of the case. "We all have a passion, all the men in this courtroom and that is to protect the womanhood of the state of Alabama," Knight declared.

However, it was Callahan's charge to the jury that sealed Patterson's fate in this case. To begin, Callahan said, "Where the woman charged to have been raped, as in this case, is a white woman, there is a very strong presumption under the law that she will not and did not yield voluntarily to intercourse with the defendant, a Negro." Therefore, the judge instructed, the jury could ignore the evidence that Price had no abrasions after the alleged act. Just having sex with a black man could be considered rape, he reminded them. Additionally, said Callahan, Patterson didn't even have to rape Price to be found guilty. He told the jury: "[T]he mere presence is for the purpose of aiding, encouraging, assisting or abetting in any way the commission of crime . . . he is guilty as the one who committed the offense, although he never moved a muscle or said a word; provided his presence did encourage, aid or cause the other party to commit the offense."

Callahan then said that Price's word, combined with consideration of the evidence, was enough to convict the defendant. Her story did not need to be corroborated by others, he said. The judge was so eager to convict that he handed the jury only the forms for reaching a guilty verdict—and not the forms for an acquittal. Only when reminded by Leibowitz of his blunder did Callahan give the jury the second set of forms.

The next day, just as the jury for Clarence Norris' trial had been selected, the preceding jury of the Patterson case reached a verdict. For the third time in three years, twelve white Southerners stood in front of Haywood Patterson and announced that they had found him guilty, and that he should die for his alleged crimes. Patterson stared at the men with hateful eyes.

Leibowitz knew he had virtually no hope of saving Norris, but he soldiered on, catching Price in a web of lies and contradictions. Again, he had to battle Callahan throughout the trial. On December 5, after the jury left to discuss Norris' fate, Leibowitz called for a postponement of the trial of Charlie Weems and the subsequent trials. He believed that his only chance of ultimate triumph would come not in Callahan's courtroom but in higher courts. Callahan, troubled by the high cost of the Decatur trials, agreed to indefinitely postpone the remaining trials.

Norris was also found guilty and sentenced to die in the electric chair. It was customary for the judge to ask for mercy upon Norris' soul, but Callahan failed to do so because of incompetence, forgetfulness, or utter disregard for the condemned man's humanity. To moderates in the region, Callahan had embarrassed the South. Stated the *Birmingham Post,* "The record of this trial, when it comes to review by the United States Supreme Court, will not be a favorable commentary on Alabama judicial procedure."

Due to the debacle in Callahan's court, and the long duration of the legal process, a sense of apathy set in among supporters of the Scottsboro Boys. An ILD-sponsored parade on December 2, 1933, attracted only eighteen hundred protestors, most of whom were Communist Party members. After sentencing, Norris and Patterson were returned to death row in Kilby Prison, while the other seven Scottsboro Boys remained incarcerated in a Birmingham jail.

But all was not lost. Their attorneys were not giving up on the Scottsboro Boys and on May 25, for the second time in three years, their cases would be reviewed by the Alabama Supreme Court.

eight

Back to the High Court

B y the spring of 1934, the Scottsboro Boys case had dragged on for more than three years, while the nine young men wasted away in jail. That spring the defense experienced a whole new set of frustrations in the Alabama Supreme Court.

Samuel Liebowitz, despite not getting paid for his services, seemed willing to carry on the defense. At the Alabama Supreme Court hearing he argued the case alongside ILD attorneys Osmond Fraenkel and George Chamlee. Liebowitz claimed that the convictions of Haywood Patterson and Clarence Norris should be set aside because black citizens had been excluded from the jury—and that names of African Americans were on the jury rolls only because of forgery. Fraenkel discussed the prejudiced nature of Judge William Callahan's trial, including his failure to initially provide the jury with forms for acquittal.

Attorney General Thomas Knight, again representing the state, argued that the court should not consider reviewing Patterson's case because the defense had submitted paperwork for a new trial past deadline. This was true—they had not filed the proper papers in time according to Alabama law—but Judge Callahan had given them inaccurate information.

Knight also addressed the issue of black exclusion on the jury rolls. He stated that it was up to the jury commission, not the Alabama Supreme Court, to decide whether a citizen was fit to sit on a jury, and the decision was based on character, morals, and other attributes. Knight did not address Fraenkel's contention that Judge Callahan was incompetent.

On June 28, in a unanimous decision, the Alabama Supreme Court denied the motion for new trials. They denied the motion in the Patterson case because the defense had missed the filing deadline, regardless of the fact Judge Callahan had given the lawyers wrong information. In the Norris case, Justice Lucien D. Gardner declared that the jury commission had not *excluded* African Americans but rather *selected* those they believed were worthwhile jury candidates. As for Callahan, Gardner said that "on one or two occasions" he had "manifested slight impatience," but otherwise he ran a fair trial.

The court set the execution date for Patterson and Norris for August 31, 1934. The defense began filing an appeal of the Norris case to the U.S. Supreme Court. However, because of the earlier missed deadline, the Patterson case had not been officially appealed to the state court. Thus, it could not be appealed to the U.S. Supreme Court. On

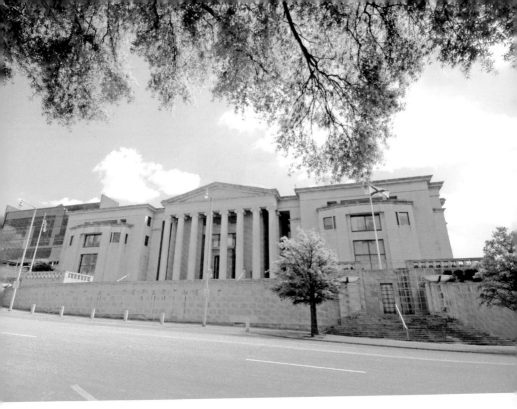

The Alabama Supreme Court building *(Courtesy of Alamy Images)*

July 9, Chamlee applied for a rehearing before the Alabama high court, postponing Patterson's execution.

Throughout the summer of 1934, Victoria Price engaged in high-stakes game-playing that would get even more people in legal trouble. In June, a representative of Price, J. T. Pearson, wrote to the ILD stating that Victoria might change her story for the right price. Attorney Joseph Brodsky designated lawyer Samuel Schriftman, under the assumed name Daniel Swift, to be the contact man with Pearson.

In August, Schriftman offered to secretly pay Price five hundred dollars to sign an affidavit repudiating her testimony. She refused to commit and in late September he upped the offer to $1,000, which she accepted. Schriftman did not know that in mid-September Price had told Huntsville, Alabama, police about the bribery and said it originated with Schriftman.

On October 1, Pearson and Price left for Nashville to meet Schriftman and an associate named Sol Kone, who carried a briefcase packed with 1,500 one dollar bills. But before the deal could be completed, county deputies pulled Pearson over and arrested him, while Nashville police apprehended Schriftman and Kone.

When Leibowitz heard about the arrests later that day, he exploded in anger. Two days later he issued a statement saying he would withdraw as the Scottsboro Boys' attorney unless the Communists cut all ties with the case. The ILD responded by dropping Leibowitz, and the *Daily Worker* smeared him as a traitor who had joined the lynch mobs of Alabama.

As in 1931, another power struggle ensued over who would represent the Scottsboro Boys. Ministers from Harlem convinced Norris and Patterson to sign affidavits transferring their allegiance to Leibowitz. However, on October 13, Norris

Samuel Schriftman, Sol Kone, and J. T. Pearson stand trial for attempted bribery. *(Courtesy of AP Images)*

and Patterson switched sides again, signing affidavits stating that they wanted the ILD to represent them in the appeal to the U.S. Supreme Court. Days later, they changed again and signed up with Leibowitz.

Leibowitz asked the NAACP to support him in his efforts, but NAACP Executive Secretary Walter White did not want the organization to get directly involved in the Red-tainted case. Leibowitz did find support from a number of African Americans in Harlem who, in mid-October, teamed with Leibowitz to form the American Scottsboro Committee (ASC). Dr. George E. Haynes, executive secretary of race relations for the Federal Council of Churches, was named chairman. William H. Davis, editor of the *Amsterdam News,* a black newspaper in New York, was named a director. The ASC declared that Leibowitz would represent Patterson and Norris. In early 1935, the U.S. Supreme Court agreed to review the case in *Norris* v. *Alabama.*

Incredibly, Patterson reverted back to the ILD again. So when the Supreme Court hearings began on February 15, 1935, Leibowitz and George Chamlee, who had cut ties with the ILD, represented Norris while ILD attorneys Fraenkel and Walter Pollak worked on behalf of Patterson.

Leibowitz, in his first-ever appearance in front of the U.S. Supreme Court, argued that African Americans were systematically excluded from the jury rolls in Alabama, and that Jackson County officials had forged African American names onto the rolls after the Scottsboro trials began. As Leibowitz explained the alleged forgery, each of the justices examined the pages with a magnifying glass.

In response, Alabama state attorney Thomas Knight said he did not know if forgery was committed, but said that careful selection was the reason that so few African Americans were on Alabama's voting rolls. This was a bold-faced lie, and the entire nation knew it—especially the nine justices sitting before him.

On April 1, 1935, Charles Evans Hughes delivered the opinion of the high court. The chief justice pointed out a startling fact about Morgan County:

> A clerk of the circuit court, who had resided in the county for thirty years, and who had been in office for over four years, testified that, during his official term, approximately 2,500 persons had been called for jury service, and that not one of them was a Negro; that he did not recall 'ever seeing any single person of the colored race serve on any jury in Morgan County.'

Hughes added that it was inconceivable that no African American citizens were worthy of serving as jurors. "[W]e find it impossible to accept such a sweeping characterization of the lack of qualifications of Negroes in Morgan County," Hughes stated. "It is so sweeping; and so contrary to the evidence."

In its decision, the court upheld an earlier Supreme Court decision, in *Neal* v. *Delaware* (1881), in which the court ruled that never summoning African Americans as jurors was unconstitutional, even if states did not have laws explicitly barring blacks from the jury pool. Therefore, Clarence Norris had been denied his constitutional right to a fair trial and "the judgment must be reversed and the cause remanded for further proceedings not inconsistent with this opinion."

Norris would get yet another new trial. But what about Haywood Patterson? The U.S. Supreme Court said it was clear that his paperwork requesting an appeal had not been filed in time. However, his case was virtually identical to that of Norris, who had just received a new trial. Should Patterson die in the electric chair over a small technicality? The high court decided to remand Patterson's case back to the Alabama Supreme Court with the implication that if that court did not overturn the verdict, the U.S. Supreme Court would review the case again.

Not surprisingly, the two sets of defense lawyers interpreted the decision differently. Leibowitz declared it a great victory for American justice; the Communists called it a triumph borne out of mass protest, not the justice system, which they said was only a tool of the ruling capitalist class.

Whatever the politics, both rulings were successes for African Americans as a whole. The Supreme Court sent a message that it would not support the corruption of the U. S. Constitution that was necessary to maintain the racial injustices and racial segregation in the Jim Crow South.

Some Southerners took notice of this slight shift in sentiment. Alabama governor Bibb Graves, who took office in 1935, said that "Whether we like it or not, it is the patriotic duty of every citizen and the sworn duty of every public officer to accept and uphold [the Supreme Court's decisions] in letter and in spirit." He added that the court's ruling in the Norris case "means that we must put the names of Negroes in jury boxes in every county in the state."

Outside the South, newspapers praised the court's decision. Below the Mason-Dixon Line, however, the reaction was mixed. Some papers remained quiet, while others ridiculed the court's ruling.

Leibowitz, hoping he had found an ally in Governor Graves, wrote him a letter asking that the state drop the case—or

Liebowitz (second from left) stands with seven of the Scottsboro Boys in this 1935 photo. *(Courtesy of AP Images)*

at least let an impartial committee comprised of clergy and university heads decide their fate. Graves did not respond.

On May 16, 1935, the Alabama Supreme Court quashed the indictments of the Scottsboro Boys. However, the defendants had little reason to celebrate because the Alabama high court also stated that all of them would be retried. Moreover, Thomas Knight announced that he had been retained by the state to run the prosecution. Worst of all, the trials would be presided over by Judge William Callahan.

nine
The Final Trials

Although they had been granted yet another chance at freedom by the U.S. Supreme Court, the Scottsboro Boys remained behind bars waiting for new trials over the next months. In the meantime, the bickering over who would represent them continued. But this time the dynamics between the dueling groups had changed.

The ILD, and the Communist Party of the USA as a whole, had a new political agenda. Soviet Union leader Joseph Stalin, threatened by the growing military power of Adolf Hitler's Nazi Germany and Mussolini's Fascist Italy, announced that the world's Communists should join forces with other socialists and leftists organizations, many of which Stalin had condemned in the past, to create a "Popular Front." This decision in far-off Moscow prompted the ILD to begin looking for a broad coalition to fight for the Scottsboro Boys.

Despite initial skepticism, the NAACP, along with the American Civil Liberties Union (ACLU), League for Industrial

Democracy, and Methodist Federation for Social Service, agreed to start cooperating with the ILD. In December 1935, they formed the Scottsboro Defense Committee (SDC) and put at its head a thirty-eight-year-old northern pastor named Allan Chalmers.

Despite his skill and determination and the fact that all the Scottsboro Boys—except the wavering Haywood Patterson— supported him, the SDC did not want Leibowitz as lead counsel. They thought he was already too hated in Alabama. Leibowitz agreed to remain in the background for the new trials and to let a white southern lawyer lead the case. Clarence Watts, a lawyer from Huntsville, Alabama, did not support desegregation, but he was convinced that the Scottsboro Boys were innocent. For a hefty fee, he accepted the case.

The trial for Haywood Patterson was scheduled to begin in Judge William Callahan's court on January 20, 1936. The defense filed a motion for a change of venue—not to another Alabama court, but to the closest federal district court. The defense contested that they could not get a fair trial in Morgan County. Respected white farmer R.A. Burleson signed a statement for the defense saying that everyone he had talked to believed the defendants were guilty. Judge Callahan dismissed the motion.

History was made on the first day of the trial: of the one hundred potential jurors brought to the courtroom, twelve were African American. During questioning, however, Callahan banned the black citizens from sitting in the jury box. When one accidentally headed in that direction, the judge declared, "Here, boy, sit over there!" Seven of the dozen African Americans asked to be dismissed from service, and the other five were rejected by the state.

The usual cast of witnesses, including Victoria Price and the defendants, told their familiar stories. But new twists developed. Former state witness Orville Gilley was in jail for robbery, and Kilby Prison guard Obie Golden took the stand for the prosecution. According to Golden, Patterson had told him that he and all the Scottsboro Boys were guilty. Though he looked sharp in his new suit that was paid for by the state, Golden did not come across as credible under cross-examination.

Throughout the trial, Callahan repeatedly snapped at the defense attorneys. After one sarcastic jab by the judge, Watts called for a private conference with Callahan and the lawyers. Watts asked for a mistrial because "the attitude of the court and the irritability the court has manifested on the bench" were significantly affecting the defendants' ability to proceed with the trial. Seething with anger, Callahan denied the motion.

Melvin Hutson, the Morgan County solicitor and a church leader in the community, made the summation for the state. "Don't go out and quibble over the evidence," Hutson brazenly announced. "Say to yourselves, 'We're tired of this job' and put it behind you. Get it done quick and protect the fair womanhood of this great state."

While instructing the jury, Judge Callahan said that if Patterson were a rapist, he should be convicted. According to writer Carleton Beals, "he glared over at the defendant in fury, his lips drawn back in a snarl, and he rolled out the word 'r-r-rapist' in a horrendous tone."

Not surprisingly, the jury found Patterson guilty on January 23, 1936. However, the jurors surprised Callahan and most everyone else in the courtroom when they fixed his punishment not at death. Instead, they handed out a seventy-five year prison term. For the first time in four trials, Patterson had a juror who fought for his innocence. Foreman John Burleson, thirty-five, a well-read, progressive-minded farmer, believed that Victoria Price was lying. Burleson compromised with the other eleven jurors, who wanted the death penalty, by agreeing to the long prison term.

On January 24, because of a delay in the Norris trial, the nine Scottsboro Boys were driven in three police cars from Decatur to Birmingham. In one car, Morgan County Sheriff J. Street Sandlin and Deputy Edgar Blalock transported Norris, Ozie Powell, and Roy Wright, who were manacled together. Outside of Decatur, Powell reached up and slashed Blalock's throat with a pocketknife. Sandlin slammed on the breaks and then shot Powell in the head.

Powell hovered near death in a Birmingham hospital, and although he later recovered, he suffered permanent brain damage. In the hospital, he told his mother, "I done give up . . . cause everybody in Alabama is down on me and is mad at me."

According to Norris and Wright, the knifing had been provoked because Blalock had berated the trio and had slapped Powell. Sandlin and Blalock, who denied any provocation, were exonerated for the shooting.

The incident complicated the entire case. In light of Powell's attack, the defense believed that Alabama jurors would be even more determined to convict and condemn the Boys to death. Chalmers believed the only hope for the defendants was to create a groundswell of support among prominent Alabama moderates. If respected Alabamians represented the defendants—and Leibowitz and the ILD were

Ozie Powell, seen here on the witness stand, attempted to kill Deputy Edgar Blalock while being transported from Decatur to Birmingham. *(Library of Congress)*

taken out of the picture—the Scottsboro Boys would stand a better chance.

In spring 1936, a white Birmingham minister, Dr. Henry Edmonds, was head of the interracial Alabama Scottsboro Fair Trial Committee. Many state figures cooperated with Edmonds' committee, including former governor Thomas

Kilby, but the group was unable to make progress. The lawyer they found was too expensive, Leibowitz refused to leave the case, and Communists continued their attacks on Alabama. By the end of 1936, Edmonds and his committee gave up.

Fortunately, state officials in Alabama were also growing tired of the fight. In meetings between Leibowitz and Alabama Lieutenant General Thomas Knight and Attorney General A. A. Carmichael, the two sides reached an agreement. The youngest of the Scottsboro Boys, Roy Wright and Eugene Williams, would go free, as would the two with physical disabilities, Olen Montgomery and Willie Roberson. Charlie Weems, Andy Wright, and Clarence Norris would plead guilty to assault but receive sentences shorter than five years. Patterson would serve no longer than Weems, Norris, and Andy Wright. Powell would be tried for his assault on the deputy.

Carmichael stated that he would discuss the matter with Judge Callahan, which made Leibowitz nervous. Predictably, Callahan strongly opposed the deal, as did Morgan County Solicitor Melvin Hutson. Then Knight died unexpectedly in May 1937. The compromise never came to fruition, and on July 12, Clarence Norris went on trial in Judge Callahan's courtroom. Thomas Lawson served as prosecuting attorney.

In addition to Knight's death, Callahan had also been ill, and the Scottsboro Boys were physically and mentally deteriorating in prison. Dr. R. R. Bridges, the doctor that examined Victoria Price, had died in March 1936. Norris' trial, held in the midsummer heat, proceeded swiftly and ended with a guilty verdict, with the jury fixing his punishment at death. The next trial, Andy Wright's, was postponed because defense attorney Clarence Watts was too ill to perform his duties. The heat, the pressure, and the hostility of his white peers had worn him down.

Leibowitz, who took the reins of the Wright case, was also at wit's end—especially after Jackson County Solicitor H. G. Bailey delivered a long attack against the attorney's home city, New York, during his summation. In his own summation Leibowitz said, "I can't fight this kind of thing. I'm entitled to an acquittal in this case . . ." The state had not asked for the death penalty with Wright, and after he was convicted the jury fixed his punishment at ninety-nine years.

In Charlie Weems' trial, Price's testimony was so full of contradictions that Leibowitz motioned that it be stricken from the record on account of perjury. Callahan denied the motion. During his summation, Leibowitz vented his frustration and anger at Alabama's white citizens. He declared that he had examined more than a thousand prospective white jurors for these trials and not one of them had said they would treat a black defendant different than a white one. Yet the whites he talked to on the streets of Decatur all said that his clients didn't have a chance of being acquitted. It was hypocrisy of monstrous proportions, he said. After his conviction, the jury fixed Weems' sentence at seventy-five years. Next up was Ozie Powell. The state dropped the charge of rape and indicted him for knifing Deputy Edgar Blalock, a charge Powell pled guilty to. Callahan sentenced him to the maximum penalty of twenty years—in addition to the six he had already served and the bullet he had taken to the brain.

On Saturday, July 24, 1937, the trials came to an eerily quiet end. Just before noon, prosecuting attorney Thomas

Leibowitz confers with Roy Wright, Eugene Williams, Willie Roberson, and Olen Montgomery after their release from prison. *(Courtesy of AP Images)*

Lawson spoke in a hushed tone to Judge Callahan. Reporters wondered what was going on. Across the street at the county jail, Leibowitz directed Roy Wright, Eugene Williams, Willie Roberson, and Olen Montgomery to hop into two cars. Leibowitz climbed into one of the cars and they drove away. Four of the Scottsboro Boys were suddenly free men.

Later, Lawson explained that prosecutors believed that the physically disabled Roberson and Montgomery were not guilty. Because the other two had been just thirteen years old, the state believed that they had served enough time in prison. However, part of the agreement was that they were required to leave the state permanently.

After more than six years, the Scottsboro trials were finally over. However, the controversy continued. If the state believed that Roberson and Montgomery were innocent, why had they served any time at all? Weren't they entitled to compensation for their six years of harsh imprisonment? Why did Norris deserve death while others got prison terms? And should the five imprisoned Boys continue to serve any more time considering the highly dubious testimony of Victoria Price?

Over the next few years, the Great Depression would end and the most catastrophic war in history would rage across the globe. Through it all, the Scottsboro case would drag on.

This illustration in the *Daily Worker* calls for the release of the five Scottsboro Boys who remained in jail. *(Courtesy of the Michigan State University Library, Special Collections Division)*

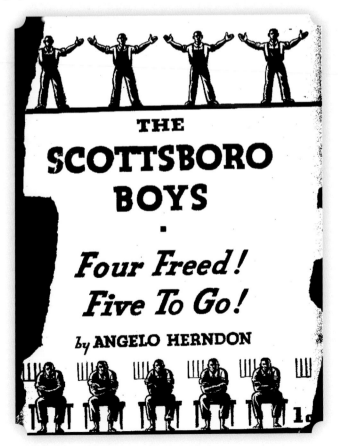

ten
Freedom

After their release from jail in 1937, Roy Wright, Eugene Williams, Willie Roberson, and Olen Montgomery went to New York with attorney Samuel Leibowitz. To protect them from hucksters, Leibowitz told them to decline all financial offers. He planned for them to attend vocational school.

However, less than a month after their release, the four young men took the stage at Harlem's Apollo Theater. Wearing fancy suits and touting canes, they appeared with a large cast of attractive women. The four enjoyed being on stage and hoped to get rich in show business. But they discovered that after one week they owed their manager and the theater more money than they had earned and went back to the Scottsboro Defense Committee for support.

Meanwhile, the other Scottsboro Boys remained behind bars, bitter that the others had been freed. On October 26, 1937, the U.S. Supreme Court declined to hear the

Governor Bibb Graves
(Library of Congress)

appeal of Haywood Patterson. However, Scottsboro Defense Committee head Allan Chalmers did appeal to the sensibilities of Alabama Governor Bibb Graves.

On December 21, 1937, Graves met with Chalmers and others to discuss granting clemency to the five Scottsboro Boys who were still in prison. Graves was told to consider the anti-lynching bill that was currently in the U.S. Congress. If he pardoned the Boys, maybe it would alleviate the image of the South as bigoted. When Graves adjourned the meeting he had not committed either way, but he inferred that he was strongly leaning toward pardoning them all except Powell.

Graves wouldn't make a commitment on the pardon until after the Alabama Supreme Court reviewed the sentences of Norris, Wright, and Weems. In June 1938, the justices affirmed their sentences. On July 5, Graves commuted the sentence of Norris—the only Scottsboro Boy remaining on death row—to life in prison.

In October, Grover Hall, a colleague of Graves, informed Chalmers that the governor was about to pardon four of the five still in prison. Powell would not get a pardon because of his attack on the deputy. They would be released from prison at 11 A.M. on Halloween. An elated Chalmers made plans, including renting a limousine to transport them to Atlanta. On October 29, however, Graves sent Chalmers a telegram stating he was not ready to act.

It turned out that when Graves had interviewed the four Scottsboro Boys in his office on the October 29, he was appalled by their behavior. According to Graves, a seething Norris—who was jealous and angry at Patterson because of a dispute over a male lover in prison—told Graves he was

Juanita E. Jackson, then special assistant to Walter White, and another unidentified woman visit the Scottsboro Boys in jail in this 1937 photo. *(Library of Congress)*

First Lady Eleanor Roosevelt was sympathetic to the plight of the Scottsboro Boys. *(Library of Congress)*

ready to kill Patterson. Patterson, meanwhile, was caught with a homemade knife in his pocket on his way to the governor's office. According to Hall, Graves said, "They are antisocial, they are bestial, and they are unbelievably stupid and I do not believe they can be rehabilitated in freedom."

After the meeting, Graves refused to grant the pardons, but Chalmers wouldn't give up. He even took his plea all the way to the White House. Through Chalmers' persistence, First Lady Eleanor Roosevelt agreed to meet with NAACP

In 1938, President Franklin Roosevelt sent a letter to Governor Graves pleading for the release of the Scottsboro Boys. *(Library of Congress)*

Executive Secretary Walter White on November 11. Eleanor then talked to her husband, President Franklin Roosevelt, who invited Graves to meet him at the "Little White House" in Warm Springs, Georgia, later in the month. Graves declined the invitation, saying he was too busy.

On November 15, Graves issued a statement denying the pardon. But on December 7, as the Boys endured another day in prison thinking that the world had abandoned them, President Roosevelt wrote a letter to the governor pleading for their release. Chalmers learned of the letter, but when he met with Graves on December 12, the governor told him he couldn't pardon the Scottsboro Boys because he would be finished politically in Alabama if he did.

Chalmers came to realize that Graves had embellished the story of the Boys' bad behavior during their visit with him. Graves' political colleagues had pressured him to deny the pardons *before* he met the prisoners, and he used the story of their bad behavior as an excuse. In late December, the spurned Chalmers went public about how Graves had broken his promise. He even distributed copies of his correspondence with the governor to reporters. Some newspapers criticized Graves, while others railed against Chalmers.

The denial of clemency closed the book on the Scottsboro case for several years. In October 1941, Weems, Norris, and Wright were denied parole, allegedly because the judges on the Board of Pardons and Parole feared that pardons would hurt them in their next election.

On November 17, 1943, Weems was finally released on parole. Norris and Wright received their "freedom" in January 1944, but the parole board insisted they work at a lumber company near Montgomery, Alabama, for extremely low wages. There they lived in one room and had to share a bed. The two eventually fled the state, violating their parole, but returned on Chalmer's advice. The parole board was not forgiving, sending Norris and Wright back to prison.

Ozie Powell finally was granted his parole in June 1946, and three months later Norris was paroled again. Patterson, deemed too surly and dangerous for society, was never

Clarence Norris leaves Kilby Prison in 1946 after receiving parole.
(Courtesy of AP Images)

paroled. However, he escaped from prison in July 1948. On June 9, 1950, more than nineteen years after the alleged rape of Victoria Price, Andy Wright became the last Scottsboro Boy to be freed.

Despite the Herculean attempts to free the Scottsboro Boys—most notably by attorney Samuel Leibowitz and SDC leader Allan Chalmers—their lives had been damaged beyond repair. Prison had been a terrible experience—vicious guards, violent inmates, disgusting food, and torturous insects. Norris described cockroaches in Kilby Prison "as big as my thumbs" that "moved in armies. They bit us along with the millions of bedbugs. The scratching that went on echoed in the night. Mice ran through the cells like pets."

These horrors took their toll.

Andy Wright, who was beaten by both guards and prisoners while incarcerated, moved to New York State after his release in 1950. A year later his former girlfriend accused him of raping her thirteen-year-old daughter. He apparently did nothing more than give her a present, and an all-white jury acquitted him—but not before he spent another eight months in jail. Wright later got married and at one point stabbed his wife, but she didn't press charges.

Willie Roberson was an asthmatic, and the filthy air of Kilby Prison aggravated his condition. During incarceration, he stated that he'd prefer the electric chair than to continue to live in prison. He died of an asthma attack.

Little is known about the fate of Ozie Powell, except that he moved to his native Georgia. However, his three months of education before the alleged rape was a severe handicap. During his years in prison, he was unable to write a letter.

Olen Montgomery, nearly blind, played the guitar and saxophone and dreamed of becoming a successful musician. However, he drank heavily and moved from one odd job to another. He occasionally relied on assistance from the NAACP.

After his release, Eugene Williams moved to St. Louis, where relatives helped bring normalcy back to his life.

Released from prison in 1946, Clarence Norris fled Alabama, violating his parole. He was arrested on several occasions, once for stabbing his girlfriend. Norris received a much publicized pardon from Alabama governor George Wallace in 1976—and was officially declared not guilty for the alleged 1931 rape. His autobiography, *Last of the Scottsboro Boys,* was published in 1979. He lived the longest, dying in 1989.

In prison, Charlie Weems was stabbed, tear-gassed for reading Communist literature, and hospitalized due to tuberculosis. Once free, he worked in a laundry in Atlanta and married. The tear-gassing continued to affect his vision many years later.

Haywood Patterson, who had initiated the attack against the white boys on the train, was the most aggressive and most literate of all the Scottsboro Boys. He was a sexual predator in prison, incurring the jealousy and wrath of many inmates. One prisoner stabbed him twenty times, nearly killing him in 1941. On July 17, 1948, while working with fellow prisoners in a rice field, Patterson escaped. He settled in Detroit, and though he was apprehended by the FBI, Michigan's governor refused to allow him to be extradited to Alabama. Patterson's chilling autobiography, *Scottsboro Boy,* was published in 1950. That December, he was arrested after a bar fight in which a person was stabbed to death. In his third trial for that offense, he was sentenced to a minimum of six years in prison for manslaughter. On August 24, 1952, he died of cancer.

Roy Wright, a sensitive boy who always carried a Bible with him in prison, appeared to make a good life for himself after his release. He joined the Army, married, and later worked for the Merchant Marine. But in 1959, after catching his wife in bed with a man, he shot and killed her—then committed suicide.

When Dan T. Carter began working on his book *Scottsboro, A Tragedy of the American South* (1969), the definitive book about the Scottsboro Boys, he wondered what had become of Victoria Price. She had disappeared, and he finally concluded that she had died in 1961.

In fact, Price was alive and well, and not yet done with the Scottsboro case. Having married twice since World War II, she had changed her name to Katherine Queen Victory Street. In 1977, shortly after the airing of the television movie *Judge Horton and the Scottsboro Boys,* she sued NBC for slander and invasion of privacy. In a California courtroom, thirty-six years after the alleged crime, Price told her story under oath for the twelfth time. However, the judge dismissed the case.

When Price died in 1982, she took with her to the grave the truth of what had happened on March 25, 1931. Most historians believe she fabricated the story in order to avoid arrest herself. Carter, perhaps the foremost expert on the case, wrote: "I am convinced beyond a reasonable doubt that she was never raped. I am convinced to a moral certainty that, as Judge Horton put it, she 'knowingly testified falsely in many material aspects of the case.'"

If Price did make up the story, then all that happened on that freight train in 1931 was a minor scuffle between white and black youths. This seemingly innocuous event erupted into one of the most explosive, prolonged, and important legal cases of the Twentieth century.

For many reasons, the case of the Scottsboro Boys is still discussed today at universities throughout the country. First and foremost, the two Supreme Court decisions that resulted from the trials strengthened defendants' rights. In *Powell* v. *Alabama,* the court determined that in capital cases—in not just federal courts but state courts as well—defendants must be given access to counsel upon their request. Subsequent decisions would strengthen the defendant's right to counsel, culminating in *Gideon* v. *Wainwright* (1963), when the Supreme Court said that defendants in all crimes must be provided an attorney if they could not afford one.

In *Norris* v. *Alabama,* the Supreme Court put the nation on notice that excluding citizens from juries based on race was unconstitutional. Southern officials would try to skirt this ruling for many more years, but by the 1960s most juries would be integrated, even in the South.

In addition to the Supreme Court decisions, the media coverage of the Scottsboro cases shone a bright light on the ugly face of Jim Crow. From 1931 to 1937, Northern newspapers, including papers that were widely read in black urban communities, decried the unjust treatment of African Americans in the South. Rallies were staged in New York, Washington, and other major cities, including some in Europe. The hugely influential *Life* magazine ran a photo essay on the imprisoned Scottsboro Boys, and Americans got to know them not as dispensable "criminals" but as unjustly treated human beings.

The Speaker of the House, vice president, First Lady, and even the president all responded to the "legal lynching."

It has been said that the Civil Rights Movement started with the *Brown v. Board of Education* decision of 1954, or the Emmett Till case, or the Montgomery Bus Boycott of 1954-1955. However, several important civil rights events preceded those famous turning points. NAACP attorneys Charles Houston and Thurgood Marshall chipped away at segregation in the courts for years and black union leader A. Philip Randolph pushed President Roosevelt to desegregate the defense industries. Adam Clayton Powell organized a successful boycott in Harlem.

Then there was the Scottsboro case, the most prominent civil rights-related case of the first half of the twentieth century. Although the Boys suffered unspeakable injustices, their case, in the long term especially, was a strong blow to Jim Crow. Ironically, the Scottsboro case revealed the rigid and fragile legal underpinning of the racial caste system in the South. It also revealed to many in the North how fearful and paranoid white leaders were. It seemed that many whites lived in such fear of interracial sex that even the flimsiest accusation of rape was enough to produce a lynch mob—and send eight innocent young men to death row. One witness, Dr. Marvin Lynch, was convinced that Price was lying, but he was so afraid of the backlash for speaking the truth that he begged out of testifying.

It also revealed how white Southerners hotly resented "outside agitators," such as the "New York Jew" Samuel Leibowitz. Whites responded to black unionization and Communist infiltration with house raids, arrests, convictions, and shootings.

Conversely, the Scottsboro case explodes the myth that *all* southern whites were bigoted during the Jim Crow period. Certainly, the vast majority were convinced of their racial superiority, or were afraid to let it be known they weren't, as evidenced by the unanimous guilty verdicts delivered in the many Scottsboro trials. However, jury foreman John Burleson, more well-read than his fellow jurors, defended Haywood Patterson's innocence during jury deliberations and some southern newspapers, most notably the *Birmingham Post,* editorialized that the Boys were not guilty. Many southern educators, legal experts, and other educated men and women believed in the defendants' innocence, even though few of them were willing to take a public stance. The story of the Scottsboro Boys is a tragic tale, filled with lies, bigotry, hatred, and ignorance. Lives were ruined, and the legal system broke down time and time again. But it is also a story of courage and perseverance.

As Clarence Norris said, after finally receiving his pardon in 1976—forty-five years after his arrest, "The lesson to black people, to my children, to everybody, is that you should always fight for your rights, even if it cost you your life. Stand up for your rights, even if it kills you. That's all that life consists of."

Samuel Leibowitz, Judge Horton, Allan Chalmers, and others put their careers and their lives on the line to fight for justice, to fight for the rights of the oppressed, and their own right to live in a country where ignorance and injustice would not be tolerated. It was through their efforts, and the perseverance of the accused Scottsboro Boys themselves, that justice, after many agonizing years, finally prevailed.

Timeline

1932	*March 24*	Alabama Supreme Court affirms the convictions of seven of the Scottsboro Boys; court overturns conviction of Williams because he was a juvenile (thirteen).
	Nov. 7	In *Powell* v. *Alabama,* the U.S. Supreme Court reverses the convictions of the Scottsboro Boys.
1933	*March 27*	Patterson's second trial begins in Decatur, Alabama; Judge James Horton presides, Samuel Leibowitz represents the defendant; jury finds Patterson guilty, sentenced to death.
	May 6–7	ILD leads a march of several thousand people in Washington, protesting the injustice surrounding the Scottsboro trials.
	June 22	Judge Horton sets aside Patterson's conviction and grants a new trial.
	Nov. 20	New round of trials, presided over by Judge William Callahan; Patterson and Norris again convicted and sentenced to death.
1934	*June 28*	Alabama Supreme Court affirms the convictions of Norris and Patterson.
	Oct. 1	ILD attorneys arrested by Nashville police for trying to bribe Victoria Price.

1935	*APRIL 1*	In *Norris* v. *Alabama*, U.S. Supreme Court overturns the conviction of Norris because Alabama officials deliberately excluded African Americans from the jury pool.
	DECEMBER	Allan Chalmers heads the new Scottsboro Defense Committee.
1936	*JAN. 23*	Patterson found guilty for the fourth time; sentenced to seventy-five years in prison.
	JAN. 24	Ozie Powell stabs Deputy Sheriff Edgar Blalock; Sheriff Jay Sandlin retaliates, shooting Powell in head; both Blalock and Powell survive.
1937	*JULY*	Norris convicted and sentenced to death; Andy Wright and Weems get ninety-nine and seventy-five years, respectively; Powell pleads guilty to assaulting Blalock, sentenced to twenty years.
	JULY 24	Charges dropped against Roy Wright, Williams, Roberson, and Montgomery.
1938	*JULY 5*	Alabama governor Bibb Graves reduces Norris's death sentence to life in prison.
	NOVEMBER	Governor Graves denies pardons to Scottsboro Boys still in prison.
	DECEMBER	Letter from President Franklin Roosevelt to Graves on the Boys' behalf fails to sway the governor.

1943	*Nov. 17*	Weems released on parole.
1944	*January*	Norris and Andy Wright released on parole
1946	*June*	Ozie Powell released on parole.
1948	*July 17:*	Patterson escapes from prison.
1976	*October*	Norris pardoned by Alabama governor George Wallace.
1977		TV movie *Judge Horton and the Scottsboro Boys* airs on NBC; Victoria Price, now known as Katherine Queen Victory Street, sues NBC for slander and invasion of priva judge dismisses the case.

Sources

CHAPTER ONE: The Train From Chattanooga

p. 11, "'The next time . . ." Haywood Patterson and Earl Conrad, *Scottsboro Boy* (New York: Bantam Books, 1950), 1.

p. 12, "Why, you goddamn . . ." Ibid., 2.

p. 12, "We had color . . ." Ibid., 3.

p. 16, "Governor as I am . . ." "The Delta," *CourtTV Crime Library*, http://www.crimelibrary.com/notorious_murders/famous/emmett_till/3.html.

p. 16, "[W]hen I was a young . . ." Beth Bailey and David Farber, consultants, *The Fifties Chronicle* (Lincolnwood, Ill.: Publications International, 2006), 87.

p. 17, "The crowd was . . ." Clarence Norris and Sybil D. Washington, *The Last of the Scottsboro Boys* (New York: G. P. Putnam's Sons, 1979), 21.

p. 17, "If those six . . ." James Goodman, *Stories of Scottsboro* (New York: Vintage Books, 1995), 5.

p. 17, "I was scared . . ." Ibid.

CHAPTER TWO: Jim Crow "Justice"

p. 24, "Name one area . . ." Clayborne Carson, primary

consultant, *Civil Rights Chronicle: The African-American Struggle for Freedom* (Lincolnwood, Ill.: Publications International, 2003), 185.

p. 26, "No jobs for . . ." Ibid., 67.

p. 26, "All Negroes Positively . . ." *Jackson County Sentinel,* March 26, 1931.

p. 27, "a common street . . ." "The Scottsboro Trials," University of Missouri-Kansas City, http://www.law. umkc.edu/faculty/projects/FTrials/scottsboro/SB_ BPric.html.

p. 27, "be out at . . ." Ibid.

p. 27, "whole bunch of . . ." Dan T. Carter, *Scottsboro: A Tragedy of the American South* (Baton Rouge: Louisiana State University Press, 1979), 14.

p. 28, "the evidence against . . ." Ibid., 17.

p. 29, "They told us . . ." Patterson and Conrad, *Scottsboro Boy,* 9.

p. 29, "I couldn't believe . . ." Ibid.

CHAPTER THREE: Death Sentence

p. 31, "Not exactly . . ." Clarence Norris, "The Great Depression: If a White Woman Accused a Black Man," Oracle ThinkQuest Education Foundation, http:// library.thinkquest.org/03oct/01794/first_hand_ accounts.htm.

p. 33, "All you sons . . ." Carter, *Scottsboro: A Tragedy of the American South,* 25.

p. 33, "Are you going . . ." Ibid., 26.

p. 34, "Victoria Price was . . ." Ibid., 27.

p. 35, "put off five . . ." "The Scottsboro Trials," University of Missouri-Kansas City.

p. 37, "They all raped . . ." Carter, *Scottsboro: A Tragedy of the American South,* 34.

p. 38, "We find the . . ." Ibid., 37.

p. 39, "Within two hours . . ." James Haskins, *The Scottsboro Boys* (New York: Henry Holt and Company, 1994), 30.

p. 40, "It is the . . ." Ibid., 31.

p. 41, "We demand stay . . ." "The Scottsboro Boys," *CourtTV Online*, http://www.courttv.com/archive/greatesttrials/scottsboro/trials.html.

CHAPTER FOUR: Communist Influence

p. 43-44, "They beat on . . ." "Scottsboro: An American Tragedy," *PBS.org*, http://www.pbs.org/wgbh/amex/scottsboro/filmmore/pt.html.

p. 45, "will kiss the . . ." Carter, *Scottsboro: A Tragedy of the American South*, 67.

p. 47, "Police Clubs Rout . . ." "Police Clubs Rout 200 Defiant Reds," *New York Times,* April 26, 1931.

p. 47, "Down with American . . ." Carter, *Scottsboro: A Tragedy of the American South*, 142.

p. 48, "one of the . . ." Carter, *Scottsboro: A Tragedy of the American South*, 90.

CHAPTER FIVE: All the Way to the Supreme Court

p. 52, "If this is . . ." *Birmingham News,* August 8, 1931.

p. 53, "Negro and white . . ." Goodman, *Stories of Scottsboro*, 27.

p. 53, "victims of a . . ." Ibid., 44.

p. 53, "These messages are . . ." Carter, *Scottsboro: A Tragedy of the American South,* 156.

p. 61, "On November 8 . . ." Patterson and Conrad, *Scottsboro Boy,* 34.

p. 61, "lie about those . . ." "Scottsboro: An American Tragedy," *PBS.org.*

p. 61, "I was drunk . . ." "The Scottsboro Trials,"
University of Missouri-Kansas City.

p. 62, "guards hated us . . ." Norris and Washington, *The Last of the Scottsboro Boys,* 49.

CHAPTER SIX: Judge Horton's Skepticism

p. 63, "It was filthy . . ." Haskins, *The Scottsboro Boys,* 54.

p. 65, "Your organization and . . ." "Scottsboro: An American Tragedy," *PBS.org.*

p. 66, "Well, they're here . . ." Haskins, *The Scottsboro Boys,* 56.

p. 67, "Judge, I looked . . ." Carter, *Scottsboro: A Tragedy of the American South,* 215.

p. 67, "I'd never be . . ." Ibid., 215.

p. 68, "said he took . . ." "The Scottsboro Trials,"
University of Missouri-Kansas City.

p. 68, "I am speaking . . ." Ibid.

p. 69, "Gilley . . ." care for that," Ibid.

p. 70, "Where did you . . ." Ibid.

p. 70, "Show them that . . ." "Famous Trials," Hugh Lauter Levin Associates, http://www.hlla.com/reference/lawinamerica.html.

p. 71, "We find the . . ." Carter, *Scottsboro: A Tragedy of the American South,* 239.

p. 72, "If you ever . . ." "The Scottsboro Boys," *thatsalabama.com,* http://www.thatsalabama.com/civilwrongs/scottsboro/.

p. 73-74, "[T]he conclusion becomes . . ." Carter, *Scottsboro: A Tragedy of the American South,* 267.

CHAPTER SEVEN: Bigotry on the Bench

p. 75, "This judge was . . ." Haskins, *The Scottsboro Boys,* 63.

p. 75, "He couldn't get . . ." "The Scottsboro Trials,"
University of Missouri-Kansas City,

p. 77, "Let's don't take . . ." Carter, *Scottsboro: A Tragedy of the American South,* 286.

p. 78, "We all have . . ." Ibid., 296.

p. 78, "Where the woman . . ." "Scottsboro: An American Tragedy," *PBS.org.*

p. 78, "[T]he mere presence . . ." Carter, *Scottsboro: A Tragedy of the American South,* 297.

p. 79, "The record of . . ." "Scottsboro: An American Tragedy," *PBS.org.*

CHAPTER EIGHT: Back to the High Court

p. 82, "on one or . . ." Michael J. Klarman, "Scottsboro," University of Virginia Law School, 2005, http://law.bepress.com/cgi/viewcontent. cgi?article=1038&context=uvalwps.

p. 86, "A clerk of . . ." "Norris v. Alabama," Cornell Law School, http://www.law. cornell.edu/supct/html/historics/USSC_CR_0294_0587_ZO.html.

p. 86, "[W]e find it . . ." Ibid.

p. 86, "the Judgment must . . ." Ibid.

p. 87, "Whether we like . . ." "Negro Jurors Are Assured in Alabama," United Press Association, April 5, 1933.

p. 87, "means that we . . ." Ibid.

CHAPTER NINE: The Final Trials

p. 90, "Here, boy, sit . . ." F. Raymond Daniell, "Negro Veniremen Appear in Decatur," *New York Times,* January 21, 1936.

p. 91, "the attitude of . . ." Carter, *Scottsboro: A Tragedy of the American South,* 343.

p. 91, "Don't go out . . ." Ibid., 345.

p. 91, "he glared over . . ." Carleton Beals, "Scottsboro Interview," *Nation,* CXLII (1936), 179.

p. 92, "I done give . . ." "The Scottsboro Trials," University of Missouri-Kansas City.

p. 95, "I can't fight . . ." F. Raymond Daniell, "Scottsboro Jury Asked to Give Life," *New York Times,* July 21, 1937.

CHAPTER TEN: Freedom

p. 101, "They are antisocial . . ." Carter, *Scottsboro: A Tragedy of the American South,* 390.

p. 105, "as big as . . ." Norris and Washington, *The Last of the Scottsboro Boys,* 177.

p. 107, "I am convinced . . ." Carter, *Scottsboro: A Tragedy of the American South,* 461.

p. 110, "The lesson to . . ." "Scottsboro: An American Tragedy," *PBS.org.*

Bibliography

Bailey, Beth, and David Farber, consultants. *The Fifties Chronicle*. Lincolnwood, Ill.: Publications International, 2006.

Beals, Carleton. "Scottsboro Interview." *Nation,* CXLII, 1936.

Carson, Clayborne, consultant. *Civil Rights Chronicle: The African-American Struggle for Freedom*. Lincolnwood, Ill.: Publications International, 2003.

Carter, Dan T. *Scottsboro: A Tragedy of the American South*. Baton Rouge: Louisiana State University Press, 1979.

Daniell, F. Raymond. "Negro Veniremen Appear in Decatur." *New York Times,* January 21, 1936.

———. "Scottsboro Jury Asked to Give Life." *New York Times,* July 21, 1937.

Cornell Law School. "Norris v. Alabama." Cornell Law School, http://www.law.cornell.edu/supct/html/historics/USSC_CR_0294_0587_ZO.html.

———."Powell v. Alabama." Cornell Law School, http://

www.law.cornell.edu/supct/html/historics/USSC_CR_
0287_0045_ZO.html.

CourtTV Crime Library. "The Delta." *CourtTV
Crime Library*, http://www.crimelibrary.com/notorious_
murders/famous/emmett_till/3.html.

CourtTV Online."The Scottsboro Boys." *CourtTV Online*,http://
www.courttv.com/archive/greatesttrials/scottsboro/trials.
html.

Faugno, Diana, Barbara Girardin, and Andrea Radoff.
"The Myths and Legends of Sperm, Sexual Assault, Sex,
and Contraception." *Forensic Nurse*, http://www.
forensicnursemag.com/articles/391clinical.html.

Goodman, James. *Stories of Scottsboro*. New York:
Vintage Books, 1995.

Haskins, James. *The Scottsboro Boys*. New York: Henry
Holt and Company, 1994.

Horne, Gerald. *Powell v. Alabama*. Danbury, Conn.:
Franklin Watts, 1997.

Klarman, Michael J. "Scottsboro." University of Virginia
Law School, 2005, http://law.bepress.com/cgi/viewcontent.
cgi?article=1038&context=uvalwps.

"Negro Jurors Are Assured in Alabama." United
Press Association, April 5, 1933.

Norris, Clarence. "If a White Woman Accused a Black
Man." *The Great Depression*, http://library.thinkquest.org/
03oct/01794/first_hand_accounts.htm.

Norris, Clarence, and Sybil D. Washington. *The Last of
the Scottsboro Boys*. New York: G. P. Putnam's Sons,
1979.

Patterson, Haywood, and Earl Conrad. *Scottsboro Boy*.
New York: Bantam Books, 1950.

"Police Clubs Rout 200 Defiant Reds." *New York Times,*
April 26, 1931.

PBS.org, "Scottsboro: An American Tragedy." *PBS.org*, http://www.pbs.org/wgbh/amex/scottsboro/sfeature/sf_ trial_1933b.html.

Thatsalabama.com. "The Scottsboro Boys." *thatsalabama. com*, http://www.thatsalabama.com/civilwrongs/ scottsboro/.

University of Missouri-Kansas City. "The Scottsboro Trials." University of Missouri-Kansas City, http://www.law.umkc. edu/faculty/projects/ftrials/scottsboro/SB_bCalla.html.

Sorensen, Lita. *The Scottsboro Trial: A Primary Source Account.* New York: Rosen Publishing Group, 2003.

Weiner, Jon. "Southern Explosure," *Nation,* May 24, 2001, http://www.thenation.com/doc/20010611/wiener/4.

Web sites

http://www.pbs.org/wgbh/amex/scottsboro/sfeature/sf_
trial.html
This link will take you to "Scottsboro: An American Tragedy,"
a special program broadcast on PBS, as part of its "American
Experience" series. Here, you'll find a synopsis of the film, a
transcript, primary sources, maps, and a timeline, as well as
audio links to the voices of participants and spectators at the
trials.

http://www.law.umkc.edu/faculty/projects/FTrials/scotts-
boro/scottsb.htm
The University of Missouri-Kansas City School of Law main-
tains this excellent site on the trials of the Scottsboro Boys. An
account of the 1931 trials, biographies, a chronology, images,
letters and accounts, and even a diagram of the Chattanooga-to-
Memphis freight train are provided on this comprehensive site.

http://www.lawschool.cornell.edu/lawlibrary/Scottsboro
Samuel Liebowitz, the attorney who defended the Scottsboro
Boys, was a 1915 graduate of the Cornell Law School and on
this Web site you'll find a short biography of him, as well as
links to other information about the trials.

http://www.courttv.com/archive/greatesttrials/scottsboro
Another excellent Web site is found here, among CourtTV's archive of "The Greatest Trials of All Time." Read about the trials (1931-1937), about the players, snd interviews, and if you have RealPlayer on your computer, you can view proceedings posted on the site's video index.

http://www.afro.com/history/scott/scotts.html
The *Afro-American* newspapers kept track of the trials throughout six years of judicial proceedings. Afro publisher Carl Murphy dispatched two young reporters to cover the trials, and on this site you will find six telegrams that they sent Murphy during particularly charged testimony. Readers will also find a chronology of national reaction to the trials, a chronology of international reaction, and yet another timeline compiled by the International Labor Defense.

http://jurist.law.pitt.edu/trials4.htm
If its details you want, visit this site. Professor Douglas Linder of the University of Missouri-Kansas City School of Law breaks down every aspect of the trials in an article titled "The Trial of the Scottsboro Boys." Linder, the creator of the "Famous Trials" Web site at the university law school, even provides an audio link to a Leadbelly recording of the song "Scottsboro Boys."

Index

Liebowitz, Samuel, *8*, *64*,
65-66, 68-72, 76-80, 81,
84-85, 87, *88*, 90, 94-96,
96, 98, 105, 109-110
Lincoln, Abraham, 19
Love, Oliver, 48
Lynch, Marvin, 35, 67, 109

Marshall, Thurgood, 109
Maurer, George, 50
Miller, Ben, 17, 41
Montgomery, Olen, *8*,
13, 13-17, 19, 27-29, 31-33,
37-41, 43-45, 47-48, 50,
52-53, 55, 57-59, 61-62, *64*,
72-74, 75, 79-80, 81, 84,
88, 88, 89-94, 96, *96*, 98,
100, 106, 110
Moody, J. E., 77
Moody, Milo C., 29, 37, 59
Morris, Luther, 35

Norris, Clarence, *8*, *13*, 13-17,
19, 27-29, 31-33, 37-41,
43-45, 47-48, 50, 52-53,
55, 57-59, 61-62, 63, *64*,
72-74, 75, 78-80, 81-82,
84-88, *88*, 89-94, 97, 99-103,
100, *104*, 105-106, 110

Patterson, Haywood, *8*, 9,
11-17, *13*, 19, 27-29, 31-33,
37-41, 43-45, 47-48,
50, 52-53, 55, 57-59, *60*,
61-62, *64*, 65, 68, 71-74,
75, 78-80, 81-88, *88*, 89-94,
98-103, *100*, 105-107, 110
Patterson, Janie, 47

Patterson, William L., 72
Pearlman, Miron, 61, 70
Pearson, J. T., 83-84, *84*
Pickens, William, 48
Pinchback, P. B. S., 21
Pollak, Walter, 57-58, 85
Powell, Adam Clayton, 109
Powell, Ozie, *8*, *13*, 13-17,
19, 27-29, 31-33, 37-41,
43-45, 47-48, 50, 52-53,
55, 57-59, 61-62, *64*, 72-74,
75, 79-80, 81, 84, *88*, 88,
89-95, *93*, 99, *100*, 102-103,
105, 110
Price, Victoria, 10, *11*, 14-17,
19, 26-28, *32*, 33-35, 37-39,
48, 65-70, 73, 77-79, 83-
84, 91-92, 94-95, 97,
105, 107-109

Rainey, Henry T., 73
Randolph, A. Phillip, 109
Reisman, Edward A., 68
Revels, Hiram, *20*, 21
Roberson, Willie, *8*, *13*, 13-
17, 19, 27-29, 31-33, 37-41,
43-45, 47-48, 50, 52-53,
55, 57-59, 61-62, *64*, 72-74,
75, 79-80, 81, 84, *88*, 88,
89-94, 96, *96*, 98, *100*,
105, 110
Roddy, Stephen R., 29, 30-31,
33, 35, 37-38, 47, 56, 59
Roosevelt, Eleanor, *101*,
101-102
Roosevelt, Franklin Delano,
72, *102*, 102-103, 109